YEAR OF MYSTERY

To Sarah

DUNCAN BASIL

Year of Mystery
Thoughts on the Church's Year

ST PAULS

Every day of the year the Church celebrates some aspect of our salvation. It may be an event from Christ's life or from his Mother's or the saints'. These celebrations make up the Church's year of the mysteries of redemption. They help us to prayer, gratitude and sometimes to thoughts such as these.

Acknowledgements: My thanks to HarperCollins Publishers Ltd for permission to use C.S. Lewis, *The Great Divorce*; Penguin Books for permission to use the Julian of Norwich quotation from their Clifford Wolters' translation of 1966.

Cover illustration: Etching by Sarah Harris

ST PAULS
Middlegreen, Slough SL3 6BT, United Kingdom
Moyglare Road, Maynooth, Co. Kildare, Ireland

© ST PAULS (UK) 1995

ISBN 085439 507 5

Set by TuKan, High Wycombe
Printed by Biddles Ltd, Guildford

ST PAULS is an activity of the priests and brothers of the Society of St Paul
who proclaim the Gospel through the media of social communication

Contents

An eternal holiday

"The feel of warm sand beneath your feet... the sigh of the sea... children laughing... a cool rush of blue-green waves... the warm breeze on your face... it's the quintessential British holiday."

(Holiday brochure)

The Bible opens with the suggestion that God was planning a kind of Mediterranean holiday for the human race. Sunshine, moon and starlight – all arranged for starters. Tame animals, green fields and fruit trees to follow; then the seaside and a climate that needed no winter woollies. And yet, at a crash this paradise of a holiday is lost.

All had been built upon one foundation, held together by the single lynch-pin of love. True love always listens, always obeys and this love was rejected. God said, "My children, as you love me, don't touch that one tree. It will only bring you endless pain. Don't touch it for it would break my heart to see you die." But the holiday was ruined because they would not listen, they would not obey. Love was rejected and the reign of fear, sin and death began.

The Father anxiously cries out, "Adam, where are you?" and the man was afraid – he hid. Now where there is true love there is no fear. Friends are not afraid of one another. Fear is the sign of alienation and Adam is now afraid of God, his Tremendous Lover.

Steadily the poison seeps down from the man to God's image at his side – "She gave me to eat." Friends do not pass the buck and now man is at odds with his helpmate, the woman. The seeds of male chauvinism and of every kitchen quarrel have been planted. They are alienated and nature itself now revolts as thorns spring up and the beasts turn savage. The very angels wield a flaming sword to bar the gates of Paradise and the Serpent lurks among the growing weeds.

It is a sorry picture and a spoiled holiday yet a gleam of hope remains. A daughter of Eve will one day mother a Saviour who will crush the Serpent's head and, in that victory, himself be crushed.

Now all this would sound like a fairy tale but for the fact that history and our own experience block such easy speculation. Thousands of years later it is the same scenario. God is here, still Love itself. The man is here though it is now God himself become incarnate. The Serpent is here, that "brood of vipers" who are plotting to murder by trickery and condemnation, "He casts out devils by the Prince of Devils." And the woman, immaculate, is also here though fearful at her Son's desperate zeal. And that far-off gleam of hope begins to shine as Christ's miracles overcome the Evil Spirit in the power of the Holy Spirit.

The background and conflict of the New Testament mirrors the Bible's opening picture of a shattered holiday. And surely our own life experience tells the same truth. Today it is man against God as legislation moves steadily against his commandments – abortion, euthanasia and violation of the Lord's Day. It is now man against woman as the divorce rate climbs to the destruction of perhaps three marriages in four. It is Cain against Abel as the world trouble spots run with blood. Our-ten-year old children have learned to murder and every D-day recalls the cost of liberty – some 40 million victims of war.

With the light of the risen Christ, the gleam of hope has dawned and he asks of us only what his Father asked of Adam and Eve. He asks us, as friends and dear children, to listen to him; only to listen to his desperate concern for our happiness in an eternal holiday. Eve did not listen as Mary did and as we must too. Christ assures us that "Whoever listens, whoever does the will of God is my brother, sister and mother". And surely that family relationship with him is a description of our real homeland where our eternal holiday first began.

8

"And the Lord God planted a garden in Eden, in the east; and there he put the man whom he had formed. And out of the ground the Lord God made to grow every tree that is pleasant to the sight and good for food, the tree of life also in the midst of the garden, and the tree of the knowledge of good and evil."

The waterfall

"And I heard a voice from heaven like the sound of many waters and like the sound of loud thunder; the voice I heard was like the sound of harpers playing on their harps and they sing a new song before the throne..."

Three nomads from the depths of the Sahara desert had been flown to France in a primitive mail plane of long, long ago. Saint-Exupery, the aviator, tells how they were taken to see a tremendous waterfall in the Alps. Water! More precious than gold in their parched homeland and here it was roaring down as if all the reserves of the world were being emptied out.

"Come, let us leave," said their guide. But they would not stir. "Leave us here a little longer." Life itself was gushing out of the mountain, the very lifeblood of all living beings. "Come." "We must wait." "What for?" "To see it stop." God must surely grow weary of such mad prodigality. It must stop. "Wait."

We submit easily to the fascination of waterfalls or the play of a fountain. Even the river of traffic seen from a bridge above a motorway can hold us entranced. It is as if something in our deepest being guesses at mystery beneath. We, like the nomads, are not mistaken for at such times we are gazing at a fundamental symbol of divinity, "Goodness giving Itself". Goodness pouring Itself out endlessly in torrents of divine life. Not lost in an infinite wasteland but caught up like the moisture from warm soil to rain down again upon the river source of these falls. We are, so to speak, watching the divine game of self-gift in love that gives and gives back again. It is the very life of the Blessed Trinity.

For the Trinity is a Niagara Falls of divine love and this we have on the best of authorities, "All thou hast is mine and all I have is yours, Father." Torrents of the living water of the spirit are flowing down from the Father to the Son and rising up again to the Source from whence they sprang. Goodness is giving itself and this is the formula of divine and Christian life.

In a sense the creation itself was a waterfall as earth, sea and sky, plants and animals all tumbled into being to praise their Creator by their form and beauty. Like a river, it is under compulsion to return by evaporation and rainfall to its source. At a deeper level we see it, not in the dumb beauty of creation but in humankind. We are the living image of God, free to make a response in the gift of self back to the Source of such love. Self-gift in love is the short formula of divine and human life. That is why, beyond analysis, we are fascinated by the inexhaustible tumble of a waterfall. This is why lovers must give and protest their very lives to each other; why praise, that glad return of thanks is so natural to us. Behind all these is the shadow of an eternal and trinitarian waterfall, of Goodness pouring Itself out and yet to be given back.

But – and it is a very big but – you can imagine a geological weather shift with rain becoming rarer, moisture returning less and less to its source until the waterfall becomes a trickle and finally is silenced. In the dry season in north Africa you can stand in a sandy river bed, a wadi, with all the evidence of a rushing torrent about you. Rocks are smooth and hollowed out, the stones scoured clean whilst green tide marks streak the wadi walls. Here is all the evidence of water with nothing to see but parched land in the burning sun. The circle of giving has broken.

Adam wanted to be "as God". He wanted to own and control all without thought of giving back and the joyous game of give and give again ended suddenly. No song of the falls, no walk with God "in the cool of the evening". The very birds have fled. The ultimate horror of God's absence hangs over us, a drought of goodness as murder, war and revenge begin to spatter the pages of the bible.

Our greed may have dried up the waters of love but behind the barrier of sin, they pile up until the dam bursts under the weight of incredible love and mercy. And this time the falls cannot fail because the return of love to its Source is made by God himself from the ranks of our own human

11

nature. "Father, into your hands I commend my spirit and all my human family with me." From a pierced Heart the waters of life are returning to their Source. It is met with a torrent of Love as the Father pours down the Holy Spirit in the mighty rainfall of the resurrection. No need now to wait until the Waterfall stops.

"The waters that I shall give him will become in him a spring of water welling up to eternal life." And for the one who believes in me, "Out of his heart shall flow rivers of living water".

Six black horses

Some time ago, listening to music in the refectory, we heard a very old and rather moving folk song. The refrain went like this:

"Madam will you walk,
Madam will you talk;
Madam will you walk and talk with me?"

He offers a "blue silk gown, to make you fine as you go to town." It earns a firm rebuff. "No, I will not walk or talk with you."

Then what about a "coach and six black horses, six black horses, black as pitch"? For a moment the song's tempo slows as she gasps at the princely offer, "Six black horses, black as pitch!" My! But "No", not even that.

There is a note of desperation in his last appeal. "I will give you the keys of my heart. Madam will you walk, Madam will you talk, Madam will you walk and talk with me?"

Her voice and the halting piano accompaniment betray that this has at last gone home. In a kind of daze she falters, "You will give me the keys of your heart and we'll be married till death do us part? Yes, I will walk, yes I will talk; Yes, I will walk and talk with thee."

The key that unlocked and gave us Christ's heart on Calvary was a Roman spear. And surely the body language of the water and the blood is asking of each one of us:

"Beloved will you walk;
Beloved will you talk;
Beloved will you walk and talk with Me?"

An old Scottish nun remembers her father singing this song to her and that was 80 years ago. She never forgot it, especially the six black horses, black as pitch.

Such a tenacious grip on memory hints at some profound truth. Can anything less than another Heart still the restless hunger of our own?

The Annunciation

When the farmer drops in to see the bursar, you can tell it a mile off as a powerful farmyard aroma enfolds him. A glance at the sky tells of the weather. A touch on the radiator... the central heating has packed up again.

Our five wits strive to tell us the truth, to make us wise. Hearing perhaps is better at it than touch or smell. But we cultivate a little deafness as the TV and radio blare away. We cease to listen.

But one person really did have a listening ear, did hear the Word of God and keep it. At the Annunciation Mary heard the word and took the Word made flesh to heart. Surely the Annunciation is the feast day of the ear.

If you should find yourself in the waiting room of a doctor who practises acupuncture – that ancient therapy of needling other people – you are likely to see on one of the walls a very compelling poster. It shows a large human ear. Now this is puzzling. It is not difficult to get the drift of a pointing finger but it is not all that easy to get the message of a human ear. Nor is it helpful to find that this ear is covered with a maze of black dots, each dot marked with the name or function of some part of the human body. One's sense of panic turns to incredulity when the doctor begins his examination by studying your own large human ear.

The theory is in fact very simple and so ancient that it would be wise to take it seriously. It holds that every part and function of the body has a direct communication with the ear; rather like the life-line that each leaf of a tree has with its roots. And so to study the ear is to study a small television screen of the human frame. Healing done in this area of the ear will have a direct access to any disaffected part of the body.

That wall poster was close to the secret of this world of ours for "In the beginning was the Word." And words were made for ears, to be heard. And since all things were created in the likeness of the Word, they too must share his word-like nature. Things themselves are words; they are speaking to us. Someone has said that trees whisper to us, trying to catch our attention. They are bursting to tell us a truth and long for an attentive ear.

And so, as we reflect on this mystery of the Annunciation, the penny drops. God, our Creator and his glorious creation are saying something, announcing some incredible good news. All depends on one thing – a ready, listening ear.

It is not that we have poor hearing. All day long noises, words, sounds are impinging on our ears often quite forcefully. The trouble is that we no longer heed them. My father used to infuriate my mother. He was deaf to her requests to carry out the minor chores of married life but had a fine ear for those asides she hoped would pass him by. It is called selective deafness and the sad truth is that most of us for most of the time hear only what we want to hear. The rest is filtered out.

"The heavens proclaim the glory of God and day unto day makes known the message..." but we like children in the market place of the world are intent on our play and "No sound, no word is heard" as Wisdom cries out to us in the streets of life. The ear has ceased to be the doorway to our hearts.

We can study the wall chart of the ear on the waiting room wall but what acupuncture could ever sort out the tangled mass of life-lines that once connected the ear to the heart?

God himself seems to have been baffled. Adam was asked "Why did you do this?" but it was no good – he would not listen. He fled to the woods, to the isolation of deafness lest he should lose his new found status "as gods". "I heard your voice in the garden and I hid..." God tries again and calls to Moses. "Here I am," he replied, "Send Aaron."

All down the centuries of salvation history our deafness has baffled divine therapy – floods, famine, prosperity, exile. Nothing works and on the threshold of salvation old Zachary is as deaf as he is dumb, desperately making signs to his puzzled kinsfolk.

15

Above all, we need a perfect listener; someone whose soul is free from the clamour of self interest; someone who can hear the Word with that intentness and absorption which amounts to total selfgift. Gabriel found just such a one in Nazareth – the Virgin Mary whose soul was immaculately free from sin and selfishness. Her ear was the gateway to her heart's total response and she just said "Yes". There is a mysterious logic about our human listening in that it conforms us to the speaker. We expect a disciple to become like his guru. Just once among the billions who have trod this earth, the Word found one person capable of real listening. Her ear was so attuned to the Father's will that the Word became flesh and dwelt among us.

It would be melancholic if that were the end of it; if this were just a past event. "History is bunk" said Henry Ford because it seemed to have no immediate effect on the production of the Model T Ford. But this mystery of the Annunciation is not simply historic – it is still at work. Mary became the one listening ear of our wall chart through which healing and life reaches every part and every age of the Mystical Body. "All generations shall call me blessed." Through her "fiat" all are now kin to her Son. The Word is implanted in our hearts conforming us into his likeness if we too listen. The Annunciation is for now.

A friend of mine, leaving our monastery after a few days visit, said, "Well, I've received the grace of my stay." "What was that?" I said. "During vespers as clear as I hear you now I heard the words, 'You are neglecting my Mother.'" I was taken aback not by the possibility of illusion – he was a Lancashire man – but that such a reproach should have been aimed at so loyal a son of the Church. Then the penny dropped. Perhaps this was a word for me and not for him; then a new penny dropped – perhaps this was a word for us all. Are we really listening?

As we ponder on this mystery of the Annunciation we might repair any neglect by asking her to do what her Son once did in the garden of Gethsemane. We might ask her to touch the ear of her servants so that our ear like that of Malchus may be healed. Then we could give a truly listening ear to the Word of God and by our "fiat" find him embodied and dwelling in our hearts.

A captured soldier once tried to hide his identity by throwing away his uniform. The enemy officer barked out a command and from long training the soldier sprang to attention, his identity revealed and his fate uncertain.

Long listening does transform us deep down. Acupuncture got it right for the ear does eventually connect with every part of the human body, for better or for worse.

"Blessed are those who hear the word and keep it." None so blessed as Mary who listened and then kept the Word Incarnate safely in her arms.

The puppy

When institutions grow, personal warmth tends to diminish. In the supermarket or in the Underground, who really cares? And yet, an ox and an ass once helped to make heaven in a stable.

Some years ago one of our monks was returning to Africa and he asked me to drive him to the airport. On arrival, we got his bags out of the van and made our way to the desk where a bored receptionist was waiting to check us in. In routine fashion she asked for our ticket, passport and visa and then motioned us to check in the baggage. It was all very impersonal and very formal. She was obviously about to switch off when my friend said. "We've also got this." And we heaved a small crate onto the scales and produced a sheaf of documents. Slightly irritated, she asked, "What's this?" "It's a dog, a puppy. It's sedated and fast asleep." The effect was electric. "Wha-a-t? you've got a dog in there? is it alive? can I have a peep?"

It was the total change of attitude that so struck me. The impersonal, formal routine of the average airport desk had suddenly dissolved in heaps. Here we were standing round that small sleeping animal, talking in whispers and peering into the crate. We were all caught up into a group of concerned and friendly onlookers. Almost instantaneously we had crossed over from high formalism into an area of warm, personal relationships. Despite the impersonal structures that must exist between airline and client, we ended up fast friends.

Since then I have had long thoughts about the causes of this surprising transformation and even now have hardly sassed it out. Perhaps more than anything else it was due to presence. As we stood there by the receptionist's desk, there was a growing awareness of the presence of a living being in this crate. And this was somehow exercising a curious charm

18

upon us. It was drawing us into a deep, shared experience. We began to smile at each other, drop our voices and masks and to talk about Africa.

The relationship began to grow as the presence was revealed. "Yes, it's a dog; an Alsatian puppy; one of the monks in Africa breeds them; you can just see it through this slot." This reminded me of the awe and reverence aroused in us by the presence of a sleeping child.

It is the "power of the innocent and the sleeping", as someone has remarked. I wondered if it was not the charm offered to us by the presence of any created thing. Perhaps the lifework of a Christian is to discern this truth, to become aware of it in every encounter. Out of such realisation grows communion with God and his creation. "Love me, love my dog; love me, love my creation; love me, love one another." Everything in the world is telling us a precious and unique truth which is drawing us into a kind of charmed circle of union and community.

Children today are learning to become "computer literate", to learn the language of this hi-tech age and become "whizz-kids". Christians have the wider scope of learning to read the book of creation. They have to become "Wisdom's-kids" and "creation literate", discerning the Cosmic Christ everywhere present.

At the airport it was a puppy and the power of its presence was evident in the friendliness that sprang up so swiftly between us. But it could equally have been the last person we met. Wisdom is crying out in the streets of the world, crying out for our faith and recognition. Baptism calls us to become wisdom's children, open to a kind of low-key wonder. It is born of the presence of Christ, the wisdom of God who is present among us in so many different ways. Maybe the shared experience of that wonder is the catalyst and safeguard of deep and enrichening community.

In a very Christian way, Hopkins says all this as he moves from the unique charm of things to the image of God, present in redeemed humanity. It could hardly be expressed more attractively than in his familiar lines:

"... for Christ plays in ten thousand places,
Lovely in limbs, and lovely in eyes not his
To the Father through the features of men's faces."

Toddler's "Yes"

There is a legend about Our Lady as a toddler, telling how she gave herself to God. The image is of a small girl, in very determined fashion, climbing the huge steps of the Temple. She is on the way to say "fiat", her first "yes". It was her total commitment to the Lord. They say that she then danced on the Temple threshold.

I have often wondered why that little word "fiat/yes" is so vastly important. It seems to have power to change eternity. It has a long history and whatever view we take of creation – a big bang or a slow evolution – it does look as if "yes" triggered it all off. "Fiat," said God, and light was made, followed by land, sea, trees. All this beautiful creation tumbling into being at this short word "yes".

On the heels of creation comes re-creation, the magic world conjured up by Mary's "Behold the handmaid of the Lord" – the "yes" of this now grown-up girl. Perhaps she learnt its power from the Father's "fiat" at creation. Did she then pass it on it to her Son against his agony in the garden? "Not my will, Father, but fiat, yes, let thy will be done..." So short a word and yet it transformed heaven and earth.

It is the kernel meaning of his words from the cross where commitment reached its climax, "Into your hands I commend my spirit... Whatever you say, Father, yes." And out of those god-forsaken depths comes its final triumph. The Father responds with the "yes" of the resurrection and we breathe again in the Spirit of the new creation.

All this hopeful and graced history seems to hang on this small word, this mustard seed of redemption. The reason being that "yes" is the touchstone of love. It is the key that opens every lock of love, when and wherever it is expressed. "I wonder if you could give me a hand this afternoon...?" "Why, yes, of course." "Do you take So-and-so to be your wedded wife?" "Yes, I do." "Do you renounce Satan and all his works?" "I do." Put Satan's "No" in any of those situations – "I will not serve" – and things fall apart. It becomes Paradise Lost.

Inevitably this "yes" will lead us to the way of the cross, step by step, at Mary's side. Love is bound to clash with a hostile world. But it brought her up the Temple steps, drew her to Calvary and triumphed in her glorious assumption. May we, through our "fiat", our "yes", win her assurance that "the Lord is with you" now and for ever.

They say that creation is really a great cosmic dance of incredible beauty and complexity. Animals, angels, man and beast all weaving the intricate pattern. "Will you, won't you; will you, won't you, will you join the dance?"

Visitation

In those days Mary arose
and went with haste into the hill
country,
to a city of Judah,
and she entered the house of Zechariah
and greeted Elizabeth.

(Lk 1:39-40)

Elizabeth, so the Angel said,
"See how it fares with Elizabeth".
    Old Zachary and Cousin Bess
      To cradle a child in barrenness;
Strange – yet stranger still for me
To cradle Christ Emmanuel
In my virginity.

      "See how it fares" – the summons
      Swept me down from Galilee,
      By Jordan's sullen stream to cleft
      And crag near Bethany.
         I stand then, at a door,
         Calling, calling
         Elizabeth.

The cry invoked an unknown breath.
It caught my cloak, swirled in a gust
That thrust me through; something leapt
And deep within a greeting, "What is this?
You visit us? Oh blest in thy belief,
Blest in thy conceiving".

But my spirit said, "Elizabeth,
Him let us bless, who visited
Our lowliness and childlessness
To rid a world of evilness.
Elizabeth, him let us bless".

                    Mother of the unborn Christ,
                    In haste from Galilee,
                    The kith and kin await you yet
                    Of his humanity.

St Joseph

*Every ten years or so in the monastery you find yourself
down for the sermon on St Joseph. You could dredge up a
previous effort but the community has the memory of an
elephant.*

*In a world of doubt and deceit he could discern the
will of God on the frail evidence even of a dream. At dead
of night, with Mother and Child, he is off on the desperate
journey to Egypt and back.*

*A craftsman is always ready to take on a willing
apprentice. We might ask St Joseph to steady our hand in
this difficult task of discernment.*

Some years ago I was spending some time on Caldey
Island, convalescing from a minor illness and on the way
home I changed from the bus, walked to the railway station
and caught a train. As we drew into Loughborough station I
reached up to the luggage rack and, with a kind of instantane-
ous despair, realized that I had left my suitcase on that bus.
And where, oh where, would that bus be now?

At this point I woke up – still snug in my bed at Caldey
with three days to go before I had to return home. But – I did
make a strong resolution to look after my luggage on the way
home. On the day itself, my friend and I were standing on the
slipway, watching the Caldey boat as it hove into sight,
coming to pick us up. And this time it was no dream.

We were both leaving for Tenby; he for a medical check-
up and I to come home. Still talking, we stepped on board
and within minutes the small knot of figures on the slipway
began to disappear behind us in the drizzle and mist. "By the
way," said my friend, "Where is our luggage?" It was not
there. An anguished shout to the skipper; a great circle of
smooth wake behind us as the boat came full turn; luggage
heaved aboard by willing hands and once more we were on
course for Tenby.

In my dream I had been warned of something quite simple and to my own advantage – but I was insensitive to the signals and muffed the whole affair. Now St Joseph had several dreams – difficult, costing and almost outrageous in their demands. Leave your home, leave your country, drop your job – and do it right now, at dead of night; wake up Mary, wake up the Child and be off. It was not so long ago since he had married his wife on the strength of another such dream, outrageous to the point of claiming an unheard of virginal conception. A few years later, when life had settled into a tolerable routine in Egypt – another such dream and another upheaval – back again, along the desert Gaza road, to Palestine. And yet another – that sent him into the obscurity of Nazareth, though his whole inclination was for Judea.

Somehow the "stuff that dreams are made on" seems too flimsy, too inadequate for such costing and tremendous decisions. Out of that weird kaleidoscope of our dream world who can say what is important and important enough to warrant the abrupt uprooting of a family and the miseries of exile? Clearly it was something St Joseph could do. He could read and interpret the signs of daily life. He had a power of discernment sensitive enough to be triggered off by dreams – even in the major decisions of life. But what of us? How, how indeed, become someone of such discernment? It was the only gift that Solomon was wise enough to pray for and maybe it is the only key to the Kingdom. It alone turns without effort through all the complicated wards in the lock of life.

Now, St Joseph was a carpenter and as a craftsman knew that it is only from long, committed experience that discernment grows. Pots made so proudly five years ago bring a blush to one's cheek today. You can mug up everything about the techniques of a craft from books in a few days but no amount of head-knowledge can bring one to this discernment, born of experience. Don't risk your neck with one who has passed his driving test – by correspondence course!

It seems almost as if craftsmanship is really a kind of obedience to the material you are working with. It takes a

26

long while to discern and respond to the faint signals broadcast to hand and eye from wood, iron, cloth or clay. It takes even longer for that obedience to become so embodied that right choice becomes second nature and sloppy workmanship a sin that grieves the spirit. "Don't creosote that," said our late carpenter, Mr Keyes, in a howl of anguish. "Don't creosote that – it's God's blessed oak."

I am told by a fellow monk, our resident Zen theologian, that the masters teach you to "live from the heart". Under skilled guidance and through much discipline it seems that a man can come to a great simplicity and this permits him to respond totally to the circumstances of life with instant discernment. If your opponent in swordsmanship is coming at you fast and furious, you don't calculate your best line of defence. That would be to limit your options. The master, who has so to speak, become discernment, simply responds with great lucidity, from the heart, to this circumstance of life. His opponent, from the dust, wonders what it was that hit him.

That was discernment in the medium of a military art but to become so discerning in so complex a medium as life itself and to be able to respond to its delicate signals with such spontaneous obedience – that must be the peak of human craftsmanship; human wisdom itself. And what of the children of God who have received the Gift, not just of human life, but of divine life itself? How live with instant docility, from a heart that is alive and indwelt by the Holy Spirit? A master-craftsman like St Joseph, is up and off into exile on the strength of a dream whilst we, for the most part, flounder in the mud of fears and doubts – though God is shouting at us loud and clear.

We take heart, I think, from the fact that we are, after all, only apprentices in this school of Christ. Whilst there are "naturals" at the work like Mary and Joseph, most of us have to learn by the normal way of craftsmanship. A call has been heard and a commitment made but it is only by constant obedience and docility to the indwelling Spirit that we begin to live from the heart. With experience, discernment grows and you begin to see instinctively that this is not square and that is not level or true. Constant response to the delicate signals of the Spirit should become second nature until, as St Benedict says, we learn to run with unutterable sweetness in the way of the Lord.

The cost of all this seems to be a kind of conversion, the sort of thing that happens when a man makes the decision to convert a hobby into his serious life's work. It means a conversion from superficial living to serious choices and decisions. But perhaps you can go further, for the flowering of craftsmanship is not so much a laborious wisdom as a kind of liberty. You get occasional glimpses of it when pots just begin to happen – they are 'born', so to speak, off the wheelhead and out of a "grave and endless play". And you wonder where they came from.

This surely is what the liberty of the children of God is all about. For the Spirit blows differently today from yesterday and you cannot respond from a book of rules. It needs something of the freedom and creativity of a well played game. But maybe only a St Francis comes through to that degree of discernment which brings such unconscious grace and beauty into the game of Christian living.

St Joseph was warned in a dream not to go back to Judea; so they went to Galilee instead and lived in Nazareth. It is worth remembering that Nazareth was a workshop where Joseph fashioned that Master Craftsman who, on Calvary, handled wood and nails as none before or since. In this workshop of the religious life, may St Joseph do the same for the likes of you and me.

Well, that was all about discernment as the vital link between vision and practical action. And if our dream is Jesus Christ, the pressing need is to know what he wants. What is his Spirit saying to the Churches, to us, to me? In any craft fine judgement comes from long and caring practice. In the craft of life, it is learnt by constant sensitivity to the call of each passing moment.

"Go to Joseph" was Pharaoh's advice to a starving people and Teresa of Avila echoed it, "Never have I prayed

to that glorious saint and gone unanswered; other saints grant particular intentions but St Joseph seems to answer them all." Discernment, perhaps included.

"Happy are those who dream dreams and have the courage to make them come true."

Epiphanies

Kings we were, settled, crowned, content,
Just the three – till a star glittered,
Crystal in the eastern air. A rift, if you like,
In heaven's tent. Too far off for certainty
But beckoning.
And though we stuck it out for some time
In pageant and the cloying toys of royalty,
In the end we went; little reckoning
How marbled terrace could spew us out
So suddenly to desert waste
And endless, endless journeying.

We came upon a king – if corruption
Crowned and squatting in some rocky
Forgotten city can claim the name –
But still he served when starlight
Failed its vital information; eclipsed,
No doubt, before such royal profanation.
He served us and
        To a queen we came,
            Golden-aureoled in Bethlehem
            For so the star, in swift descent
            Of courtesy, revealed her – a mother
            Of maidenhood enhanced and unassailed
            By the Child, asleep, asleeping
            In her lap.

Gold to Golden Infancy we gave
And frankincense though acrid it seemed
To fragrance of that virginity.
Myrrh, too, though none of us knew why,
And to this day we wonder, though somehow
It seemed fitting.

Strange how desert sand and desert thorn
Petalled and sang
To our homeward, sandalled feet.
But dust, these palaces,
To dust these caparisoned walls,
To dust have fallen – against that hour
When yet again we meet.

Seldom by starlight
Comes the call from our father's land;
But Gentile, Magi blood in us
Quickens, assents and leaps
To an Epiphany
We sense and understand.

The Magi

At Christmas there is the crib, the manger, the Mother and the Child. Crowded in with them are the shepherds, the ox and the ass. But we still have to leave room for three more yet to come – the Magi.

On the feast of the Epiphany they stand silently in the stable. We seem to recognise intuitively our pagan ancestors and wonder at the mysterious charm of these and other gentiles in the scriptures.

There is about the Magi something of the child; a kind of simplicity that goes straight to the heart of the matter. "We've seen his star in the east... where is he? Hang all this midrash business, all those commentaries. Where is he; he must be somewhere? This King of the Jews; we've come to adore him." It is the simplicity of childhood which, like the Emperor's new clothes, is oblivious to the surrounding consternation. Herod was very touchy about any new born king. "He was troubled and all Jerusalem with him."

It adds up to a direct, uncluttered assent to truth and their response is equally forthright – a simple "yes". They saw a star; they journeyed on; they bowed down and adored; they opened their treasures and went home by another way. The child or the stranger can see things in a fresh light often denied to the expert and these Magi are scriptural kith and kin to us; simple, loveable, direct. We can be proud of them.

You notice this simplicity throughout the Bible and it touches a hidden nerve of compassion in us. "Where you go, I go too; where you die, I die too," said the alien Ruth. "Say but the word and my servant shall be healed" said a Roman soldier; "even the dogs eat of the crumbs from their master's table" was the witty reply of a desperate foreign mother and, of all people, it was the pagan NCO in charge of the execution squad that blurted out, "truly this was the Son of God".

All these gentiles of our family tree, leapt to an assent, they said "yes". They were, so to speak, "naturals" for truth.

We too have seen a star and with their simplicity have come to the crib for one thing alone – to adore. It is true that their pilgrimage, like life, was a kind of search moving towards journey's end. But life is ultimately all about adoration. It is a response to a presence; not a movement but stillness and an opening of the heart to offer gifts. Love's golden obedience, prayer's silent incense and the myrrh of sharing his bitter pangs.

The danger is to sneak back to the old ways, to the old city of sophisticated, comfortable ways; to Herod's foxy and devious pleasures. Back to the old ways of minds, hearts, rooms and days all cluttered up and, like Jerusalem, troubled; the star no longer to be seen. Surely this feast is saying to us, "blessed are the pure in heart for they shall see God" even in a little Child, even in a stable.

In a sense it is the feast of Mary whose gaze pierces to the truth of this small human bundle and rejoices in God her Saviour. And these Magi, these Gentiles, our dear ancestors, have come from afar, like us, to the crib... simply to adore.

Candlemas

A young, rustic couple coming to the Temple to present the Child to the Eternal Father. Eight days old and yet begotten before time began. No wonder they stand marvelling as old Simeon foretells the future of this "Light and Revelation for the Gentiles".

This is a feast of giving, a feast of presenting a most precious gift, a child totally given and offered up. The feast lingers on in the mind probably because it is lit by candlelight. Somehow that bowl of small, glowing candles goes right to the heart of this mystery.

They were alive with living flame and human warmth as we processed around the cloisters. Sympathetic to the touch as you peeled off, from the back of your hand, a blob of hot wax or held the slender column that bent slightly in your warm grasp. Homeliness seemed to glow from their special light as it reflected off the faces they illuminated – a truly enchanting radiance.

But candles touch this Marian mystery more deeply than this graced homeliness. Our candle warms, lights and cheers at the total expense of itself. It burns itself out; has nothing else to give. It has shared its living flame with those going home in the dark procession of life. At the end of the feastday nothing remained in that once glowing bowl. Truly a presentation of all that is most dear – a holocaust of waxen flesh, of wick and living flame.

Mary, on this feastday, probably lit no candle; but virginity, like a flame, burns without loss. She burned, warmed and lit the way for others. It was a presentation of all she held most precious. A child in arms in the Temple; a corpse in arms at the foot of the cross, when all was over and done. But a light not extinguished. Now she burns brightly – a beacon for us until we come home, living flames, like candles to the great bowl of heaven.

Saints would burn themselves out for God. If only we could sanctify in some graced way those derisive lines:

> My candle burns at both ends,
> It cannot last the night;
> But, ah my foes and oh my friends
> It gives a lovely light.

John the Baptist

The saints in heaven do not forget us nor have they lost the power to help us in our necessities. Each saint in his own special way. St Anthony still finds the keys of the car and St Jude still copes with hopeless cases. But John the Baptist surely tops the lot. He shows the way, points out and reveals to us the Lamb of God, the Christ – the One who, as the Light of the World, should be the most obvious presence on earth. All along the winding paths of life and through our deserts of fear and doubt, St John is ready to point out the One standing unknown perhaps in our midst.

On top of an overhanging rock, the little fox was really enjoying life. "Little fish, little fish", he taunted, "If you don't find water, you'll die." And the panic stricken tiddlers darted off to Mum – "We'll die, we'll die if we don't find water." And Mum, growing frantic, joined in the general panic.

"You know," said a wise old man, "when you come to write your next essay, don't be afraid of stating the obvious." Now you would think that there could be nothing more obvious in this world than the presence of God. "Ever since the creation of the world, his invisible nature, namely his power and deity, have been clearly perceived in the things that have been made."

This suggests that things were originally created, not to distract, but rather to reveal, to make manifest this presence of God; to be attractions rather than distractions. Each mortal thing must bear within itself some likeness to God since before creation there was literally nothing else for them to be like. God was the only blueprint, so to speak. If only we would, if only we could open our eyes to the obvious – perhaps we should see him everywhere, looking at us, full in the face. But what, what indeed, has gone wrong and how on earth can it come right?

Perhaps the Garden of Eden gives us a clue. Before the tree blossomed, before apples were around, Adam and Eve must have been the world's first and most continuous contemplatives. Land, sea and sky; animals, trees and plants... all were revealing "him who made us" and calling for recognition, admiration, wonder and praise. A procession, not of distractions, but of attractions and thanksgiving – as one thing after another reminded them of their dear and familiar friend.

But then came the apple. Desired for its own sake and no longer as a gift and witness to its Creator, it became for our parents, poisoned fruit. It blotted out their vision of God. For self-love imposes its own terrible conditions – it blinds our power to see things as they really are. Something easier to experience than explain. For instance, sheep and frolicking lambs are, to a butcher, so much meat on the hoof; this field of golden rape seed – just pots of honey to the average beekeeper. Self-love blinds and Adam shattered the mirror of creation with the apple and, with it, the reflection of the face of the beloved. "He was in the world and the world was made by him and the world knew him not. He became flesh, came to his own people, he dwelt among them and they gave him no welcome, they received him not." "Is not this the son of Joseph, the carpenter?" How then shall we poor banished children of Eve come to see again the obvious; how find this water in which we live and move and have our being; how find the face of God once again reflected in this world about us?

That little fox, in case you had forgotten him, is still around. "Little bears, little bears if you don't find the air you'll surely die." But he reckoned without Mother Bear. "Shut up, you brats; go and stick your heads in a bucket of water and you'll soon find out." Mother Bear seemed to grasp intuitively that a short cut to the truth, to discovering the obvious, is to experience the shock of its opposite. To realise air, try the bucket; to come to illumination, live for a while in darkness; to discover the other, forget yourself.

And that perhaps is the significance of John the Baptist (I had not forgotten him) because wherever there is this sudden discovery of the obvious there is going to be shock. It shatters complacent views until, amidst confusion, the truth is revealed.

In the midst of the routine offering of incense, suddenly there is an archangel at the altar's right side and Zachary struck dumb; Elizabeth's barrenness is defied and the unfamiliar name of John scrawled across a wax tablet to the consternation of the villagers. What make of this lad who opts out of village life and vanishes in camel skin and girdle to the desert to live on honey and locusts.

How cope with his clamour "make straight the ways of the Lord"? How penalize this layman who calls the clergy of his day, not "Your Grace", "My Lord" but "You brood of vipers"? Consternation and shock wherever John appears and all compressed and expressed in his refrain, "Repent, change your minds, open your eyes and see the truth, the most obvious truth in the world" – "Behold the Lamb of God who takes away the sin of the world."

He was not thinking of his own sin for Our Lady had seen to that at the Visitation. She brought to him, as yet unborn, the Lamb that sanctified him in his mother's womb. But John's sinlessness is perhaps the secret of his charism, his special gift to make known the truth, the obvious truth. If self-love blinds, he being sinless, was therefore free of it. He could see. He could discern, cry out, point out what others could not see, though standing in their midst. Sinless, John's heart was pure and blessed are the pure of heart for they shall see God and they can reveal him to others. "Ecce Agnus Dei... See, there is the Lamb of God."

Incidentally, the fox is still around but now he has aged and practical jokes have hardened into cruelty. That fox Herod gave a banquet, the main course the Baptist's head, its tongue stuck through by the needles of the king's vengeful queen. John in death is still at his life's work of shaking us awake and the shock of that banquet still has power to rock us; to open our eyes to the cruel reality of our fallen state, to our need for the Lamb who conquers.

Surely John's grace for us, today, is this. To show us the obvious and to win for us the grace and power to see, to contemplate his cousin, Our Lord, the Lamb who takes away the sin of the world. He stands in our midst, the Word, present in everything... in sacrament and sacrifice; in persons and things; reflected in the mirror of creation.

"Look, only look," says John, "And see the truth, the only truth, the obvious truth; the Lamb who takes away the sin of the world."

All of which flows easily into verse!

THE DESERT EPILOGUE

You may ask, Why the desert;
  asp and scorpion scattered
  dried as the locusts,
  hot as the bees,
  bereft of rock –
   stocked honey?

    Could all that matter
     against the scariness
     of village life.
   What none could see, I saw.
   Confronted, livelong day,
    by the bones of things,
    their naked being –
  even
    their Triune destiny
    when he had come
    to set them free.

      How live when reality
       seemed hallucination
       to villagers around me
       and I, the blind,
        decried for my stupidity?

Only One knew why.
    Knew why infinity
    should blaze from stone
    tree and starlit sky.
Only she and I
    the secret shared. And why?

        Immaculate before conceived,
            her cry gave me her purity
            and power to see
            as pure in heart alone can see,
            the Majesty
            in creation's imagery.

            But for the desert,
                clean, empty, solitary,
            eyes had dimmed
                and missed the moment,
                Ecce Agnus, Ecce, Ecce, see.

The Baptism of the Lord

The baptism of Jesus in the Jordan takes us aback. Can you purify innocence? But really it should cause no surprise for hints are being dropped throughout the Bible.

"O come to the waters all you who are thirsty – it's free; so come." On opening the bible we come to strange foreshadowings of Christ's baptism in the Jordan and the descent of the Holy Spirit upon him. Look at page one of Genesis and there you find the Spirit brooding over the waters of chaos – another dove and other primeval waters.

Turn on and there again you find the dove and the waters. Noah is stretching out his hand over the flood to receive the dove, an olive branch in its beak. In that olive branch is a hint of salvation, of bodily safety and life to come. A foreshadowing of the far off redemption.

Turn to the New Testament at Christ's baptism and there once more you find water and a dove. Here are the waters of Jordan, still symbolic of the chaos of sin. They flow on, like life itself, to the Sea of Death. Here again is the dove hovering over the waters, still the harbinger of peace, the life-giving Spirit of the creed. Here now is "My beloved Son in whom I am well pleased." Why so pleased? Because he is like us sinners in all things, save sin.

That little phrase, "save sin", makes all the difference because you cannot cleanse the innocent, as John the Baptist strongly protested. But this sinless one can cleanse the guilty. He can reverse the downward spiral of the old testament types of chaos and deadly floods. He can wash clean and sanctify the waters because the power of the Spirit-dove has come to rest on him for ever. Chaotic waters of sin can no longer cover the earth; flood water can no longer imperil our salvation. The Jordan need no longer sweep us along the river of life, down to the Dead Sea. Sanctified waters, baptismal waters, now bear us up to eternal life. From now on, all water is holy and boiling a kettle or washing up have become grace-full actions.

You can measure the power of Christ's baptism by its effect on the growing Child. Before his baptism he is the child of the crib; infinite yet an infant; Word of God but speechless. As a growing boy, he the almighty, is subject to Mary and Joseph. He made the world and yet for thirty years remains unnoticed as an obscure carpenter – "Can anything good come out of Nazareth?" But after baptism, as he emerges from the waters and the dove descends, notice the transformation for this is what should happen to us at baptism.

This obscure workman is now empowered to fast forty days in the desert; to fight, in an agony of temptation, the Prince of this world, the strong man whose power so far has remained unchallenged. Christ comes back from the desert in power to proclaim the good news against all opposition; to cast out devils, to heal the sick and to raise the dead. Perhaps, most marvellous of all, he is empowered to face willingly, lovingly a Roman crucifixion and carry it through to the resurrection and beyond.

Such is the power of this baptism of the Spirit, who hovers over the waters of the Jordan. All down the Christian centuries the same dove has hovered over the baptismal font. Today that same power is offered anew in this eucharist as we meet with this beloved Son on whom the dove descended. No wonder the Church cries out, "Oh come to the waters all you who are thirsty for eternal life. Though you have no money, come."

"If you knew the gift of God and who it is who is saying to you, 'Give me a drink,' you would have asked him and he would have given you living water."

A lift in Lent

"Coming events cast their shadows before" and that is the stark truth of Lent. The Passion darkens the horizon and seems to mock the hope of resurrection. We badly need a lift in Lent.

The coming event may be a dark shadow – the thinning of the ozone layer with cosmic disaster to follow or it may be a bright shadow.

"Daffodils that come before the swallow dares
And take the winds of March with beauty."

There you have a bright shadow: flowers and birds foreshadowing the approach of summer, nature's promise of a glory to come.

"Coming events cast their shadows before." Holy Week is almost upon us – a struggle of death and life, of darkness and light, of horror and of joy. Small wonder if its shadow falls on us now, flickering between brightness and dark as we listen to the Lenten readings.

Only a few days ago Peter had heard those chilling words – "Get behind me Satan" and then the first, shocking prediction of the Passion – scourging, mocking, spitting, crucifixion. Dark shadows cast by dark events to come.

But another unique, unheard of event – the resurrection – also casts a shadow. It is the bright shadow of the Transfiguration. Mount Tabor was the timely event demanded by the approaching darkness. If ever Jesus and his disciples needed encouragement, it was then.

Christ, wearied by the dusty roads, drained by the healing power that went out from him, misunderstood by friend and foe alike, crucifixion now inevitable – Christ needed that encouragement, that affirmation: "You are my beloved Son; even your dusty, travel-stained clothes are radiant in my sight." The Transfiguration has cast the bright shadow of Easter on earth's most precious child.

Those fearful apostles, dragging behind on the road to Jerusalem, desperately needed this affirmation. They needed to see that face, not beneath a crown of thorns, but radiant in glory. Peter's dreamy comments show how consoled and encouraged they were, "It is good for us to be here."

As Lent begins to bite, we who live in the darkness of faith need a glimpse of the reality and goal of our heart's desire – the glory of God in the face of Christ Jesus. In dark times it is hard to believe that our homeland really is in heaven or to believe that he will transfigure these wretched bodies into copies of his own glorious body. Well, the Transfiguration is the bright shadow of the resurrection – his and ours – bringing to our workaday world comfort and joy.

How shall we receive, how come into such glory? It's very simple, really. Abraham in faith said "yes"; gave his assent to God. Three simple, costly letters – YES. There was Isaac his only beloved son, bound to the wood of sacrifice, yet Abraham said, "yes" – as Mary would say "yes" and her Son in the garden say "yes". Coming events cast their shadows and they knew, as we know in faith, that Lent's trials are a matter of days but transfiguration and resurrection are for ever. During Lent, let us, whatever the cost, simply say "YES".

Lent is the old English word for Spring. You could call it the Holy Week of Nature when life arises out of wintry death. Like swallows, like daffodils, the Transfiguration casts a bright shadow and gives us the lift we badly need in Lent.

Waiting for the Spirit

An unforgettable experience of blind flying comes when,
after lurching up through black, rain-sodden clouds, you
break through into the dazzling sunlight, into total calm
above the carpet of cloud beneath you.

Sunday by Sunday we recite in the Creed, "He ascended into heaven and is seated at the right hand of the Father." It comes trippingly off the tongue but does it really come home to us – just what do we believe? For all that a Bishop of Durham might say, Our Lord was seen to ascend, to leave the earth. The wisdom of this lies in the fact that his departure had to be seen, had to be witnessed. If not, there would have been endless rumours of his being concealed somewhere on earth, still alive and haunting the centuries like the myth of the Wandering Jew. "But," says that dratted bishop, "we know that the world is round and that there is neither up nor down, that heaven can't be 'up there'; up for the English would be down for the Aussies." But surely Scripture got it right, "He ascended into heaven". It states a definitive departure and carries with it powerful overtones.

At every Mass we hear the old "sursum corda" "Lift up your hearts" and we respond "We lift them up to the Lord". We are affirming our resolution to follow the ascended Christ; to rise above ourselves and turn our hearts towards heaven, towards our heart's desire. As we do so, something important begins to happen. We ourselves begin to rise above all that on earth looms so large and forbidding; above all the walls that divide and sunder us; above the clouds of doubt and despair; above our resentments and into the sunlight of God's peace and calm.

This is a time to ascend heavenwards to our real home for we are, after all, only temporary dwellers on this earth. The Ascension is trying to strengthen a nostalgia, a homesickness for Paradise. It is that awareness of the transitoriness of this beautiful but sorrowful creation. Philip Sidney put it well in one of his sonnets.

"Leave me O love that reachest but to dust,
And thou my mind aspire to higher things;
Grow rich in that which never takest rust,
Whatever fades, but fading pleasure brings."

As Christ left them, his parting words were to wait for the power of the Spirit from on high. "To wait." A hard task now that earth is bereft of his presence. For waiting is not easy. We have all stood on a rail platform on a Sunday afternoon; no restaurant open; no papers; no books. A cold, down at heels waiting room; two hours before the next train and you stare at the rusty gasometer across the track through blurred and grimy windows. We are waiting, and the average waiting room bears all the signs of mortality – a place for killing time.

Yet, despite the tedium and loneliness of waiting, all the ingredients of love are at work in the hearts of a waiting man. There is faith that a train will come, that home can at length be reached; there is hope that family and friends will be there in greeting – not just the chill of an empty house. In waiting there is love, an attraction stronger than the pull to pack it all up and go back to town, to the warm conviviality of a pub. Love's call resists and puts home and family before self-satisfaction. The heart of a waiting man is the heart of a lover.

So, after he has ascended, blessing us as he ascends, we wait – nursing a curious sense of being forlorn. Could there really be such another Comforter as Jesus; could there be any substitute for the Heart that so understands our worries; for the Healer of our bodies and souls; the Shepherd who so resonates with our sorrows? Well, a lover's heart believes all things, hopes all things, endures all things. He has said wait for the Comforter and our Ascension-time task is to find the best conditions for waiting.

The disciples waited in an upper room, in a place of quiet – in the dear company of Mary. They were "all together", praying because you can't demand a gift. You can only long for it and hope for it. Upon this praying and waiting group the Gift of the Spirit at last descends.

The station may be desolate; the waiting room grimy; the gasometer looming large but a lover's heart is always lifted up. Despite the cloud that caught him away from their eyes, despite the finality of his going, they went back to Jerusalem with great joy and were continually in the Temple blessing God. On Ascension day, "Sursum Corda" seems to be our watchword; lift up your hearts for Christ is ascending and where he has gone we, after waiting a little while, hope to follow.

Pentecost

"Nothing of him that doth fade
But doth suffer a sea-change
Into something rich and strange."

(W. Shakespeare)

On opening the Bible at page 1, it is rather disappointing to find that the earth does not begin with a Big Bang. Equally disappointing to find that it does not start with creation out of nothing. Clearly something is there already in a fair state of chaos which some believe is the mess left by the revolt and fall of the angels. On the whole it looks as if "change" or "transformation" would better describe that miraculous transformation as the Spirit broods over the face of the waters and this beautiful world emerges into the sunlight of the first day. All is moving, of course, to that climax when, out of mud, the Spirit brings the flesh and blood image of the living God – Adam, the "man of earth".

You would almost expect such a transformation since he is the Spirit of love and we know from experience that love does transform, does bring change. Lovers begin to think alike, act alike and eventually, like Darby and Joan, to look alike. "The characteristic of the Holy Spirit's action," said an old pastor, "is change."

When the Spirit came upon Samson he changed and tore a lion to pieces like a young kid. The Spirit touched Jeremiah and his childish "Ah, I'm too young for the job" gave way to the crucified likeness of Jesus himself. By the Spirit's over-shadowing, a Virgin became a mother, the human mother of a Divine Child. That child, once the Dove has rested upon him, emerged from a hidden life into the power and glory of his ministry and passion. Finally comes the ultimate, impossible transformation when he rises from the dead to breathe upon us that same Spirit. And we, by Love's magic become children of God; muddy flesh and blood transformed, changed into children of God.

But the opening pages of the Acts are as baffling as the first page of the Bible. When the fullness of time has come and a Man has come back from the chaos of death, things seem to misfire. Christ has risen but the Apostles – definitely not. And this is strange since they had had a total experience of the Saviour. They had seen his miracles, heard his teaching, cast out devils, healed the sick and received the sacraments; yet look at them – nothing has changed.

They would not believe. "And this the third day since it all happened..."; doors are locked in fear; "Are you going to restore the kingdom now?" Thomas doubts and the risen Christ rebukes them all at table for their craven unbelief. They really are the same old cup of tea, unchanged because the Spirit of love has not yet cast out fear. Despite our alleluias, there is a kind of pathos about paschal time – Christ is risen but as yet the Spirit has not descended upon our chaos.

Jesus of course realises this, realises that redemption is not yet complete and simply tells them to do nothing. "Just wait, wait in the city until you are baptised with the Holy Spirit." Without the power sent down by the Father, they are power-less, still very muddy flesh and blood. Then, as the house rocks in a gale of wind and the fire descends, that ultimate transformation occurs. Things really do change. Children of wrath become children of God as the Spirit is poured into their hearts. Servants become friends, no longer slaves but sons. St Paul dares to call us other Christs, "I live, now not I, but Christ lives in me..." With that go all the gifts and charisms that so characterised the first disciples. The Spirit is a wind of change, bringing an in-depth transformation. Christianity is not a laboured imitation of Christ but possession of his Spirit, the pneuma, and he is a divine power like the compressed air of pneumatic tools. When a Spirit-filled Samson met a lion, the lion never knew what hit him. The power of the Spirit had come upon him as it would upon us at Pentecost.

But "Brothers, what shall we do?" How shall we enter more deeply into this transforming event? It is an unchanging question that receives from Peter, the first Pope, an infallible answer. "You must repent; be baptised and receive the Holy Spirit."

How repent? Well, it's not a hurried "I confess"; the crowd was "cut to the quick." Why? Because an eye-witness had held up to them the horrific mirror of sin. "This Jesus whom you crucified..." Look steadily into that mirror, realise that I did this, and repentance is born. Peter went out and wept bitterly. Should we do less?

"Be baptised." Can we enter again into Mother Church's font and be re-baptised? Just think of the early Church's baptism where a radical choice was made for Christ. You plunged beneath the water, a "No" to the old way of life. You emerged rising to the new life of the Spirit, a radical "Yes" to God. But a fat smile spreads over our face as we recall our own baptism – "You can't repeat baptism!" But alas, we sin, we grieve the Holy Spirit – or to put it bluntly, we leak like a punctured tyre. And this is serious. Our Father's work needs spiritual power because he asks us asks for more than good intentions. We are being asked to succeed in the work he has given us to do. Sin hinders our efforts and we must ask the Father to give us, as St Luke promises, his gracious Spirit.

Repent, be baptised, receive the Holy Spirit and let Pentecost change us into his likeness. Praise will well up and community form. Christ's healing power will go out from us because Christ's love has transformed us. He has given us the gifts, fruits and charisms of the Spirit as tools needed to do the Father's will.

To sum all this up. The Spirit brings deep sea-changes. The Bible does not open with a bang but with seven days of silent, beautiful transformation as he broods over chaos. By his power the heroes of the Old Testament were fitted for their role – a Samson, a David, a Jeremiah. Even after the resurrection, the Apostles must wait, idle and powerless... "I am going fishing," said the bored St Peter and caught nothing. Until the fire falls, they are powerless to proclaim the good news that changes children of wrath into children of God. Repentance, baptism and the reception of the Spirit open the door to the whirlwind change of our lives. With

Mary and the disciples in the upper room of Heaven we can wait, praying for his coming and then, with power, go out to spread the Good News.

Change is the silent message of the seasons hinting at the rhythms of another world.

Peonies for Pentecost,
Roses late in June;
Daisies due at Michaelmas
Then Autumn — ah, so soon.

Autumn must to golden dust
The Summer's sudden fling;
And Winter steal the treasure-trove
To squander it on Spring.

Should a Spring forever last?
Its blossom ever bloom?
A Summer season endlessly
Outwit a Winter's gloom?

Beauty cannot frozen be,
Nor Truth to stillness come
Their roots are in divinity,
A dance of Three in One.

Risen for me?

"Godhead here in hiding whom I do adore..." Truly he
seems a hidden God and the resurrection almost too far off
to speak powerfully to me today.

It is still paschal time but Holy Week seems centuries ago.
The altars were stripped, the tabernacle left empty and the
shadow of Lent hardly dispersed. It seems years ago that the
blossoming pear tree outside my window was black and bare
with the snow lying thick on the lawn beyond. Since then
everything has been insisting in a crescendo on the Resurrection. Alleluias past counting; paschal candle; flowers and
white vestments – all speaking of the joy of the Risen Christ.
Since then snowdrops, crocus, daffodils, swallows and just
recently, the cuckoo. It is spring, telling the same story that
death is not the end. Christ has come to give us the impossible dream of eternal life, our childhood's dream of living
happily ever afterwards.

The message is loud and clear but does it speak to me? In
my small world has he risen for me? In this day and age it is a
difficult message to believe. Doctors are still baffled by the
mystery of death and sickness is still with us. Besides, it all
happened a long time ago and seems a bit remote, a bit unreal
in this humdrum, workaday world. Like the apostles, fears,
doubts and perhaps a feeling of unreality all swirl through our
minds. Christ is risen, but is he risen for me?

Probably we have not noticed it, but the Church has been
offering us day by day the antidote to this malaise. She has
been giving us the gospel accounts of the Easter appearances
to disinfect our minds of indifference.

These texts give the lie to our fears and doubts. The
disciples were full of the fear of death, hiding behind locked
doors, locked like our hearts... and yet he stood in the midst
of them, alive and breathing peace into their fearful hearts.
Thomas doubted as we may doubt but "see my hands and

feet" and his doubting has became a spur to our belief. It triggered off the ninth beatitude that so reassures our hearts. "Blessed are those who do not see and yet believe." To the disciples, as to us, he seemed unreal, possibly a ghost, but a ghost does not eat broiled fish or boast of flesh and bone. To them he seemed as absent as he may seem to us today – but, on the way to Emmaus, two of them found a third person walking at their side all along the road of life.

Does he still seem far off? Well, here on the altar – "This is my body, this is my blood"; here in our very hands and our hearts. That close. Can he still seem so far off?

The Church's liturgy has not been deceiving us; nor the happy witness of spring around us. Christ is alive, here and now, alive with the spirit of truth soon to be poured out anew on us at Pentecost. We have only to believe to find that Christ has indeed risen for me.

"Do you really believe all that nonsense?" said my agnostic friend and turned back to his treadmill of weary unbelief. Of a sudden I saw the greatness of the gift of faith.

Road to Emmaus

"While they were talking and discussing together, Jesus himself drew near and went with them. But their eyes were kept from recognising him."

(Lk 24:15-16)

If the stranger in the story of the road to Emmaus had turned out to be Lazarus and not Jesus, I think we would have felt a bit creepy – a corpse called back from the dead, a man still mortal and destined to die again. But that is not the message of Easter. It is Good News, not a creepy story because Jesus has risen to a glorious existence free from the limitations of space and time. He is no longer subject to death but is the same yesterday, today and for ever. Lazarus might have been an eerie companion but Jesus radiates glory and joy. The story assures us that he is with us in every walk of life... "I AM the resurrection", here and now, I am with you always.

His task on the road of life is to turn us around. He wants to get us, like the disciples, heading back to Jerusalem, to the real and eternal Jerusalem. It would be an almost impossible task if baptism had not given us the faith to believe. The wisest men of Athens laughed Paul to scorn when he mentioned the resurrection and a recent poll showed that some 70% of Christians were reluctant to believe in this mystery as a real event. Perhaps we make it more difficult by a kind of laziness about our faith; a laziness that Christ had to rebuke even in the first generation of Christians. "O foolish men, so slow to believe..."

We are lazy perhaps because our companion on the road is so demanding. There is nothing more draining that laying down one's time and life for others – though it is the condition of resurrection. But he comes to our rescue. He knows how to bring us to the point of "pressing him to stay" until, in faith, we say "Stay with us Lord for evening is coming on."

He does this by drawing us to the scriptures and the reason is simple. Before plain facts, before stark reality we usually cave in and stop resisting. And the scriptures are rock bottom about the reality and destiny of this world. There is nothing like the word of God to bring us to a recognition of the Word incarnate and so to believe that he is with us all along the road of life.

Such living faith can make signs very significant and at Mass they speak with power. Jesus, as at Emmaus, takes bread – life's symbol; breaks it – the shadow of death; and gives it – eternal life shared with us. We by faith recognise his real presence as did the two disciples, their hearts burning even though "he then disappeared from their sight."

With this stranger, recognised now as the risen Lord, we can turn back to the new Jerusalem with renewed faith, proclaiming that "the Lord is risen indeed and to this we all bear witness."

Doubting Thomas

"What is faith? It is that which gives substance to our hopes, which convinces us of things we cannot see."

(Heb 11)

There is something reassuring about Doubting Thomas. Somehow his doubts find an echo in our own hearts for, after all, seeing is believing and dead men tell no tales. If only we too could have seen him alive and touched his wounds ... how strong our faith would be. We find it easy to go along with Thomas, to resonate with his obstinate reasoning.

And yet Jesus is very firm with St Thomas and with us. "After all, the Pharisees saw me and did not believe; Pilate saw me and doubted Truth incarnate standing before him; I was silent before Herod and mockery was all I got." Christ closes off these tempting thoughts because only faith can penetrate the good news of Easter. Physical sight can see the stark fact of a crucified man talking, eating and drinking as if nothing had happened but faith alone goes to the heart of the matter.

Faith alone tells us that this very man is the Son of God, risen now in glory, living outside space and time, no longer subject to death. He is free to pass through the locked doors of the upper room and free to pass through the locked doors of our hearts. It really is a time to echo those words of the Exultet: "Oh happy doubt of Thomas that provoked the Risen Christ to leave us those immortal words... 'Blessed are those who do not see and yet have believed'."

This vision of faith may seem very costing to us as we tap our way home like blind men through the streets of life. But just see, for a moment, how faith really does bring us into the glorious liberty of the children of God. Just watch it at work.

Mary Magdalene sees a gardener until the touch of faith wrings from her, not Rabbi but Rabboni, a title in Hebrew that has overtones of divinity. Or again, two disciples on the road to Emmaus sit down with a stranger and then, on a sudden, recognise the Lord in the breaking of bread. Doubting Thomas might simply have said, "My Lord," when Christ appeared like Lazarus from the dead. But faith is given and he can now confess... "My Lord and My God." The vision of faith has made possible his proclamation of the Good News just as it did for St Peter – "You are the Christ, the son of the living God."

The vision of faith is costing and we also may want to see and touch the risen Lord but in that one simple phrase we are given the golden key of eternal life... "My Lord and My God." That is enough; for "Blessed are those who have not seen and yet have believed."

Thomas doubted and Peter denied and both are now in glory. Our own moments of doubt and denial may yet serve us as stepping stones to heaven.

The Ascension

Like the Assumption, this feast tends to baffle us since we have little inkling of what happened next. Our Lady quietly left us for heaven and a cloud caught Jesus out of sight from the apostles... and then?

If creation somehow bears the mysterious likeness of God, Three in One, then perhaps all earthly things are hinting at the significance of his ways with us. But you would hardly have expected space travel to come up with answers.

Someone recently lent us a magnificent book of photos taken by astronauts as they gazed down upon our world. Beautiful photos of earth seen as a bluish and radiant sphere, floating in the blackness of space. There were photos of the Grand Canyon; of the whole Pacific Ocean and photos of towns and villages on this small planet Earth.

But the book was more than a collection of photos. It was also an anthology of texts in English, French, Arabic, Japanese and other languages. Astronauts of many nations were all describing in their own words the impact made upon them by these awe-inspiring views. And they testify to a single strange fact – that if you gaze down from a great height upon this planet you will never be the same again; you will be a changed person.

Somewhere between 80,000 and 100,000 feet, as you rocket into orbit, it happens. You suddenly see, no longer the launching pad, the countryside around it or the continent you have left behind a few seconds ago – but the whole earth. You see this mysterious sphere, floating, incredibly, silently, unsupported in space. Even the most staid and objective flight engineer is taken aback. He breaks out, over the radio, into at least 40 seconds of poetic astonishment at the majesty, the colours and the harmony of this our workaday world when seen for what it is – a single harmonious and precious whole.

This experience seems capable of transforming even a cool and objective technician into something more human. He seems to move from sheer delighted astonishment into a realization of the fragility of this dear and homely earth. And this in turn gives way to a sense of concern for its perilous beauty. Ultimately compassion for earth and all its children becomes the common experience of these astronauts from so many nations. They have even formed an international club to share this strange enlightenment, born of their vision of earth from above.

I wonder if there are not profound resonances between the mysteries of this earthly earth and those of the kingdom of God who created all things and stamped them mysteriously with his likeness. After all Julian of Norwich, moving in the orbit of a spiritual vision, was shown this world "no bigger than a hazel nut, lying in the palm of my hand... as round as a ball... I thought that because of its littleness it would suddenly have fallen into nothingness... and I was answered... it lasts and always will, because God loves it, and thus everything has being through the love of God... and he is the creator and the protector and the lover."

Astronauts and Julian were both moved to compassion for the fragility of this dear creation and maybe this is a special grace of the Ascension... it is more than a stepping stone to Pentecost or a fitting end to Our Lord's life on earth. It is also an assurance of Christ's overwhelming compassion as he takes his last glimpse down on this so very fragile and threatened planet. Remember how he raises his hands and blessed it. Then ascending into heaven, at the Father's right hand, he pleads with compassion for its healing and consolation.

The Fathers of the Church say that the Persons of the Trinity looked down with compassion on the chaos and misery of this earth. Taking council together, the Word accepted his Father's plan to come and dwell amongst us.

By dying and rising from the dead he would then give the new life of the Holy Spirit to those living in the darkness and shadow of death. Divine compassion was the motive and its vibes were felt even by the astronauts as they looked down with such concern on this war-torn and eco-threatened world.

Fundamental option

It went something like this. "Good master, what must I do to gain eternal life?" "Keep the commandments." "And then?" "To be perfect, sell all you have, give to the poor and follow me."

Consternation! No wonder. It looks as if the new law of Christ weighs more heavily than the old law of Moses, with all its 600 do's and don'ts. Yet Jesus insists that his burden is light and his yoke is easy.

Years ago I had a New Zealand friend, much loved but constantly irritating because he would keep on asking, "Why?" "I am going shopping." "Why?" "Because I've got nothing for supper?" "Why?" "Two friends called in for a meal yesterday." "Why?" And on it would go. He was, as the jargon goes, interested in fundamental options, the basic choices of life. He was, in fact, echoing the scriptures, "I have set fire and water before you; life and death – put out your hand to which you prefer; choose".

For some mysterious reason we can say "no" to eternal life and that is a fundamental option leading to death. By the help of God's grace, we can say "yes" and that leads to life, to a happiness in heaven such as no eye has seen, no ear heard... things beyond the mind of human ken. But this "yes", this most fundamental of all options seems to grow more and more difficult, almost impossible, as the old law gives way to the new – as Christ replaces Moses.

Just think of that fearful litany of Christian conduct which the gospels promote. Jews were forbidden murder and we are forbidden its first step, anger. Who has not been angry during this past week or even day? Hell seems to lie in wait for the Christian who calls his brother a fool – perhaps the commonest word in our gossip about others; the old law forbade the breaking of an oath... and we must not swear at all, even perhaps at the kitchen cat.

No wonder a famous novelist remarked, as he left the font after his reception, that he felt bowed down by the weight of responsibilities heaped upon him by Mother Church. The new law seemed heavier than the old; the fundamental option more radical, more depressing, the "yes" of Christ infinitely tougher than the "no" of Moses. Henceforth no anger; no name calling; no oaths. Sell all and give to the poor.

In a sense the novelist was right because Jesus is less concerned with the fruit of the tree – the rotten apples of an angry word, the leering glance or the occasional oath. Christ wants to pull up the roots of vice, not pluck its fruits; he wants to change the heart itself, that invisible source and root of all fundamental human options.

You may ask what power on earth could effect such a transformation, such a U-turn. Just think about it. What power could stop wars: make the police unnecessary? What could close the law courts, open prisons and consign locks and chains to the museums? Love alone could do it. It would need the power of a universal love that preferred to give rather than receive; to welcome rather than repel; to heal rather than wound; to bless rather than curse.

Such a power of love is precisely what Christ has come to give – the new heart of the new covenant. Christianity is not simply a stricter form of the old and impossible law. It is the gift of the Spirit of love itself. He is the only power which can enable us to do the impossible business of loving God, others and ourselves. "Where there is love there is no labour," said St Augustine, "or if there is labour, it is loved". This was the power and joyous mood of Easter when the risen Christ first breathed his Holy Spirit on the disciples. It is the same Spirit he now offers us in the eucharist – the power to do the "impossible".

St John Chrysostom said that after Holy Communion we should be like lions breathing fire, the fiery power of the Spirit. Here is the strength to choose life rather than death; to say "yes" rather than "no". If he dwells in us we can take that fundamental option of seeking first the kingdom of God and of making light of the crosses on our pilgrim way.

The Sacred Heart

In late spring when the birds are singing, the sun shining and the bees humming away, you notice a worried looking monk. Why worried? "Well, I've got the sermon for the Sacred Heart," and a thousand misgivings are troubling him. Too sentimental; out of date devotions; THAT kind of piety or the fear of being thought a sacristy louse — as the French so elegantly put it. All fair enough but our devotion these days is pretty thin. We hardly turn a hair at the great mysteries of our salvation — the word made flesh; Christ dead and buried or this is my body, this my blood. During the rosary we wonder what's for supper.

Much of which is head knowledge whilst the heart sleeps on and we drift into a world that forgets it has forgotten God. If we are to become more human and learn to live again from the heart, maybe we need to swing back to something more personal and loyal than cold facts and rationalistic theology. Here then is an attempt to take a new look at the very ancient devotion to the Sacred Heart.

"My true love hath my heart and I have his,
by just exchange one to the other given;
he holds mine dear and his I cannot miss
there never was a better bargain driven.
My true love hath my heart and I have his.

His heart in me keeps him and me in one,
my heart in him
his thoughts and senses guide;
he holds mine dear for once it was his own,
I cherish his for it in me abides.
My true love hath my heart and I have his."

I have lived with that poem for a long while now and still do not know if Sir Philip Sidney was writing a love poem or expressing some deep spiritual commitment, amounting to an exchange of hearts. But these lines and the impact they make do seem to validate the use we make of the word "heart" as the basic symbol of our human lives.

In the face of so much sentimental art, or restrained by the stiff British upper lip, we do perhaps try to avoid the word as much as we can but for some words, "primordial words" as Rahner calls them, there is no substitution. If you try to define them you diminish them – the heart is in fact a "muscular circulating pump" just as the hand is a "corporal grab instrument" but neither description even guesses at the real profundity of these basic word-symbols of us who are made in the image of God.

Of all such words the "heart" does seem to reign supreme, indifferent to race, to place and to history. Br Gerard, a visiting monk from Provénce, quite unbidden, chiselled a heart on my brother's gravestone. Recently I noticed it carved onto a bench at a country railway station. Richard Coeur de Lion, the Lion Hearted, springs fresh from the pages of history and many centuries before Christ, David's heart was knit to that of Jonathan's. And then, at Mount Sinai, in the most radical use of the word, in the first commandment itself, "Thou shalt love the Lord thy God with all thy heart..." – a command re-iterated by Jesus himself who obeyed it to the uttermost. So for today, "If you should hear his voice, harden not your hearts," for, as someone has said, "In the scales of God, hearts alone have weight."

Since the institution of this feast much has gone by the board – the 40 hours watching before the Blessed Sacrament, the litany of the Sacred Heart with its haunting melody, and even the statues have vanished. There remains here only a faded red badge in our bee-house that has sustained us bee-keepers in our perilous occupation. But it would be cata-strophic, it would turn us into stony-hearted Pharisees, if we let sentiment or commercial piety quench the central message of this mystery, expressed in a symbol that has served our human race so radically and so faithfully for so long.

This Sacred Heart, even in its crudest representations is assuring us beyond our hopes and dreams that we are loved with an immense and burning love despite the wounds our sins and ingratitude have inflicted; despite the cross, the crown of thorns and the mortal thrust to the heart. And because love is a two way affair, "a better bargain driven", this infinite love of Christ for us thirsts for only one thing – our love in return, love for love. "How can we fail to love One who has so loved us?" said St Bernard.

The message is the more urgent for us in that the circumstances that evoked such a powerful expression of Christ's love have intensified beyond belief since the day of St Margaret Mary in the seventeenth century. The coldness of Jansenism that transformed God from a Father into a ruthless tyrant, hell-bent on our ruin, together with the secularization of society that made his presence redundant – all these have evolved into the final blasphemy of "God is dead." No longer to be feared, no longer to be taken into account in the affairs of men, "He is dead"; a matter of indifference, that very indifference which kills love and prompted this desperate manifestation of God's love in the symbol of his heart.

He showed me his divine heart. "Behold this heart which has loved men so much that it has spared itself nothing, even exhausting and consuming itself in testimony of its love. In acknowledgement I receive from most men only ingratitude, by irreverence and sacrilege and the coldness and scorn they have for me in this sacrament of love... I ask that the first Friday after Corpus Christi be... a special feast in honour of my heart, when reparation and amends be made to it; and communion received in atonement for the indignities to which it has been subjected while exposed on the altars..."

It may be that bad art and secularization have done their work only too well and if we wish to re-discover our devotion we shall have to go back to origins. I am thinking of St Mechtilde and the warm, friendly community of her monastery of Helfta. The peace and tranquillity of that contemplative house seems to have made possible a much more amiable and wondering relationship with the Sacred Heart. You do find the same insistence on the cross, on the need for reparation but less of the anger, the reproaches, the wrath of God's justice. It seems that among friends praise and thanksgiving are that much easier. And the setting of Mechtilde's visions can ease us into a greater appreciation of this mystery because they so often take place in those liturgical and biblical events that go to make up our own monastic life. "One Sunday while they were singing the Asperges, Mechtilde said to Our Lord: 'My Lord, with what wilt thou now wash and purify my heart?' Then he with inexpressible love leaned over her, as a mother over her son, took her into his arms and said; 'I will wash thee with the love of my divine heart'; he then opened his heart, treasury of divine mercy, and she saw therein a river of flowing water. It was the river of love. Her soul plunged into it and at once it was cleansed from all its stains."

The Divine Office and the familiar pattern of our monastic day can perhaps draw us to this loving Heart more naturally than the rather pietistic devotions of litany, 40 hours and the apostleship of prayer.

So far our search has taken us to Margaret Mary of the seventeenth century and to Mechtilde of the thirteenth but since Vatican II most of us have felt the impulse to go even further back, back to origins, back to sacred scripture itself.

Almost inevitably we find ourselves standing, with the Mother of Jesus, there at the foot of the cross, at the very source of today's mystery. Here is the same message that Margaret Mary was to proclaim centuries later – for here was a heart that had loved men to the uttermost and yet in return had received only ingratitude; the thrust of a spear, the more poignant for being aimed at one defenceless in death. And here, too, man's brutality provokes not anger but this mystery of love in which death itself cannot obstruct Christ's self-giving for "there came forth blood and water". Blood from the heart of the Lamb that was slain and water springing up from within as the priceless gift of the Spirit; blood of the eucharist and the water of baptism. From the right side of the temple of his body, a river of Spirit-life springs, broadens and deepens till it reaches us here and now. And we, perhaps, by our indifference wielded the spear that struck him.

What a heart that answers such aggression with love and reveals the very mercy and compassion of God himself. And what a heart that offers itself again and today, longing that we in our turn will offer our own hearts whole-heartedly to him.

"My true love hath my heart and I have his;
by just exchange, one to the other given.
He holds mine dear and his I cannot miss,
there never was a better bargain driven."

Well, that was meant to be a corrective to our stiff-upper-lip spirituality and perhaps to something of the Pharisee in all of us. The call is to greater warmth in our relationship to Christ, to each other and to ourselves at a time when most pictures and statues of the Sacred Heart have joined old furniture in the attic. Such a devotion clashes with the prevailing non-committal attitude of "feeling free" or the indifference of "God is dead". To regain a human heart maybe there is need to be soaking up more scripture; to be more aware of Christ's presence in the eucharist and to contemplate those five wounds once so dear to English piety. In any event, not forgetting St Teresa's desperate plea – never to become distanced from the humanity of Christ with the Heart as its centre.

Love your enemies

The toughest nut in the Christian menu is surely forgiveness not just for kith and kin but for enemies, too. Cats versus dogs, red rags and bulls, wolves and sheep – all these scarcely hint at the "impossibility" of Christ's clear command. A victim shake hands with his mugger? A smile for the blaring stereo next door? How cope, how forgive even one's enemies?

Thank heavens that Christianity is more than uplifting words. It is the gift of the Holy Spirit whose power can crack this toughest of nuts.

Christ seems to turn the Old Testament upside down for it is no longer an eye for an eye and a tooth for a tooth but "love your enemies; love those who persecute you". And he speaks so plainly that there is no wriggling out of it. "Your heavenly Father pours down blessings of sunshine and rain on friend and foe alike... you must do the same." He seems to turn the old law upside down and in so doing offers us a very tough challenge... love your enemies.

But the logic of it is very simple. If you want to make something, a table or a woollen jumper, you look for a pattern or reach for the DIY book for an image of what you want to make. And God did just that. He made us, as Scripture says, in his own image and likeness. In our case he himself was the pattern, the model and here, of course is the snag. God is Love.

If we really are in his image and likeness, then we too should be all love, all generosity, all kindness to friend and foe alike. In a word, loving our enemies. A good model imitates its original as a model car to some extent does what a real car does. God is love and his image should love. We human beings should be a glorious race of mutual service and affection – machines, if you like, with a built-in disposition for love.

But we know the reality – an eye for an eye, a tooth for a tooth. We know all about crowds being mowed down by machine guns, about car bombs, Lockerbie, muggings and the violence that smoulders within our hearts. God is love and his image was built to love. Yet we, like the first children in the Bible, turn on each other. Cain slays Abel and a generation or so later a man demands vengeance seventy times seven for the enemy who strikes him. So desperate is the situation that God himself comes in person to set things right. "The Word was made flesh and dwelt amongst us, full of grace and truth." And he showed us, in a world of hatred, how this loving machine, this image of God, should go about its god-given work.

"Love your enemies" and he submits willingly to the kiss of Judas; "offer the other cheek..." and the soldiers beat him over the head with a stick and spat on him; "If someone orders you to go a mile..." and he went willingly the endless mile of the way of the Cross. "Pray for those who persecute you..." and he prayed, "Father, forgive them for they know not what they do." In a word, he was perfect in loving as his heavenly Father was perfect. He loved us to the uttermost.

If all this were just a magnificent example of how we should love ... then I think we would despair. Our best resolutions snap like dried twigs and once again it is an eye for eye or a mugging in our streets. No. The good news is that Christ came to give us the strength of a new and divine life. As the risen Christ, he comes in this Mass to make us children of God who is love. We are now empowered by the Holy Spirit to do the "impossible thing" of loving even our enemies.

The going is tough. It is hard work bending and straightening out the crumpled metal of a crashed car but the power is given. For starters, we can follow up his instructions by praying for those who persecute us. And it does work. Remember the great quarrel that flared up between St Peter and St Paul – "I withstood him to his face", said St Paul and it nearly was a tooth for a tooth. But prayer prevailed and our two saints became perfect in love as our heavenly Father is perfect.

A mysterious and ancient tradition holds that the executioner is saved if forgiven by his victim. Both together will come to walk the golden streets of Paradise. It happened at Calvary and it is happening to us.

5000 for dinner

*Christ, in a desert place, promised bread to 5000 hungry
people, bread that would come down from heaven. It
would be food to give eternal life. Childhood stories insist
that the only acceptable ending is "to live happily ever
after". Anything less – 10 years, 20, even a 100 – would
just not do. The shadow of death would still cloud the
happiness for which we long. And this is the promise of the
eucharist, eternal life – to live eternally and happily ever
afterwards.*

M any here this morning may have at the back of their
minds the thought of today's dinner, Sunday's dinner.
Mothers are probably anxious; have they set the oven control
just right? Fathers and the rest of the family are simply
banking on it. And if dinner today is roast lamb, then already
it is hinting at mysteries beyond itself – the Passover lamb,
the Last Supper and even at this morning's eucharistic meal,
where we encounter the very lamb of God.

Years ago a dozen or so of our family would gather at the
long dining room table – father at the head and mother at the
opposite end. I do not know what you do now in these days
of fast food, but in those days father would carve the joint,
the plates would be passed up to mother, each one named as
it was handed on – Enid's, Mick's, Paul's. Mother would
then add potatoes and veg accordingly. I used to wonder at
what seemed to me a slow and rather cumbersome way of
serving but age has taught me its secret wisdom.

Food is life and lack of it is starvation, death. This little
family ceremony was reminding us that our parents, who had
first given life to the children, were now, out of love, sustaining that life in us. Father carved the joint and Mother added
the veg and we, the children, blissfully lived on.

But we lived on in a special kind of way for, as someone
has said, we do actually become what we eat. This gift of food

had the power to sustain in us a *family* likeness. Not any kind of likeness but one special to each family since every child knows that there is no cooking in the world like mother's; no Sunday dinner like hers.

Well, God is a father, our father, and he who first gave us life is concerned about sustaining it. So, he too is interested in food for his family. Manna in the desert; then the Passover lamb to seal his first covenant; then the last supper to institute the new and eternal covenant and here, today, the representation of that covenant-meal in this holy Mass, this sacred banquet.

Our Father, through his Son the lamb of God, has given us not merely life but eternal life. He has prepared this eucharistic meal with great love and at great cost. He has gathered us round this table and not by chance – for each one of us is named.

And he, together with his Son, hands us the food to sustain the everlasting life which he first bestowed on us in baptism. His aim, through this meal, is to refashion us evermore in the family likeness of his Son. For heavenly food, above all others, empowers us to become what we eat; to take on the likeness of Christ.

Food, too, has a mysterious quality that we seldom think about – it is meant to be shared and therefore to bring about unity, communion. It is life and like a candle flame you can share it without loss; light a thousand other candles and yours is as bright as ever. Life and food are for sharing – so much so that I once met a French theologian who was writing a learned thesis against self-service. It was morally wrong, he held, since self-service was entirely directed towards helping oneself. It was closed to others and had nothing of sharing about it; nothing of love and therefore nothing of life. Self-service was simply not Christian.

Christ, then, breaks the bread so that it may be shared, so that the good news of eternal life may be proclaimed and celebrated beyond the walls of any one family, of any one building. It is not to be stockpiled as a kind of food-mountain, useless in its isolation.

And the feeding of the five thousand gains clarity and

meaning in the light of today's Sunday meal. Life, eternal life, is sustained by the manna of holy Communion; family likeness to Christ and his mother is etched more deeply in us. And living unity, the fruit of sharing any meal, is promised us now and then, "happiness ever afterwards".

There are sermons in stones, said Shakespeare. He might have added – there are sermons, too, in our Sunday dinner. Let us hope that the oven control WAS set just right.

Taxes to Caesar

Its "heads or tails" to settle life's minor decisions but seldom has a coin carried such a fundamental option as that denarius, that coin of the realm to be "rendered unto Caesar".

"Should we pay taxes to Caesar or not?" The general drift of today's gospel is that Our Lord has very shrewdly avoided a trap – give taxes to Caesar, worship to God. We are body and soul, earth as well as spirit. Earthly kingdoms and the heavenly can both claim their due. Christ has upheld loyalties to church and state. The Pharisees cannot accuse him of treason to Caesar or of blasphemy against God. "Give back to Caesar what belongs to Caesar – and to God what belongs to God." He has escaped the trap.

A lesser known interpretation of this passage harks back to the Garden of Eden, though it gets lost by translation into inclusive language. God said "Let us make man in our own image and likeness." So, when God in Christ asks for a coin, he sees the head of the creature he had created – a man. He then speaks words once used in the garden. Whose "image and likeness" is this?

He is saying, perhaps, "Yes, the State has its just claims on you; pay your taxes... but an image belongs to the craftsman who fashioned it. You belong to God. You are His image and likeness, so give back to him what is his ... yourselves." He is inviting the Pharisees to repent, to give themselves back to the Messiah as he tries to gather them under his wings... and they would not. St Thomas More, you remember, made this self-gift magnificently; "I die the king's good servant, but God's first."

The offertory of the Mass gives us daily the opportunity of giving back to God what belongs to God, the "image and likeness" that is our very selves.

Fathoms deep below the surface storm of taxation is the mystery of our self-gift to God, our fundamental "yes" or "no". A decision for eternity too huge for the casual toss of a coin.

The Pharisee and the publican

The author of the Oxford English Dictionary obviously knew his Bible. In defining hypocrisy he echoes the words of today's parable: "Hypocrisy is the assuming of a false appearance of virtue or goodness, particularly with regard to religious life or belief."

Jesus "spoke to some people who prided themselves on being virtuous and despised everyone else." Hypocrisy is not a nice vice. We don't like to own up to it and yet it clings to us as close as a wet bathing costume. As we listened to the Gospel, we were, perhaps, thanking God that we were not like that dreadful Pharisee; perhaps wondering if we would care to be seen in the company of that vulgar publican. A young couple remarked to their vicar that they no longer went to church since church-goers seemed no better than the rest of us. "Your church, Vicar, is cramfull of hypocrites." "Not quite", he replied, "I think there is room for two more."

This assuming of a façade of goodness seems as natural to us as breathing. Not really surprising since hypocrisy is there from the start of the human race. "The woman you gave me to be my companion," said Adam, "tempted me and I ate." The woman, also looking virtuous, passed the buck; "The serpent beguiled me and I ate." The devil had promised them they would be "as Gods", immortal, omnipotent, immaculate and they were trying desperately to keep up the pretence, to maintain that false appearance of virtue.

And the devil is still at it and we are still at it. The other day, in a magazine, I came across the devil's beatitudes, not Our Lord's, but those of the primal serpent, still plying his trade. Here are just a few:

Blessed are those who are too tired, busy or disorganised to meet with fellow Christians on Sunday each week; – they are my best workers.

Blessed are those who claim to love God and at the same time hate other people; – they are mine for ever.

Blessed are those who have not the time to pray; – they are easy prey for me.

Blessed are you who, when listening to this, think it is about other people and not about yourself; – I've got you already!

Centuries after the Fall, Our Lord was tackling this same weed of hypocrisy, flourishing as ever – "how is it that you want to take the splinter out of your brother's eye and not see the plank in your own?" Today it is still growing strong despite all the weed killers and pesticides employed by Mother Church. An old cantor remarked to me that whenever he had to tell someone that he was singing flat in choir, he invariably got the reply, "Me. Singing flat? You should hear the man next to me."

Is there an instant remedy, a wonder drug, some antibiotic for such a deep-rooted malady? Is there a way truly to be humbled and be exalted with God's friends for ever? Well, only a plumb line will show if a wall is vertical; only the petrol gauge tells if the tank is empty and only the cross tells the truth, the whole truth and nothing but the truth. It is a mirror and to gaze into it is to see the truth, the truth about myself; that Christ died for sinners.

The cross mirrors at a glance the false assumptions I may have about my own goodness – there, on the cross, but for the compassion of Christ, go I. It is an instant remedy for hypocrisy and forces from us that cry of anguish, "Lord be merciful to me a sinner".

In the Mass, we stand with Mary at the foot of this terrible mystery; convicted and yet joyfully convinced that "all who humble themselves before the cross will be for ever exalted with Christ in glory".

77

Passing by

A blind man sitting by the roadside, calling out in desperation for healing. Would the young rabbi stop or would he pass by? The whole human race seems caught up into this fearful moment – will he stop or pass on and pass us by?

St Mark's story of blind Bartimaeus interests us – not so much for its very human overtones – the crowd tells him to shut up; then, changing its mind, cheers him on – it interests us because it seems to touch some inner nerve of the heart. Something stirs in the half-asleep world of our faith.

That we need healing, some sort of serious eye surgery for our spiritual blindness, none would doubt. But beyond such healing something else is nagging away – probably because this text is more than a healing account. It is also a "call" story. Matthew, at a call, got up from his money table; Peter left his nets and this blind man throws off the cloak of an old way of life – to follow the call, all along the road, all along the way, probably to Calvary itself. Disciples have heard a call.

A nerve is touched because deep in us there is the "wild call, this clear call that may not be denied". We are created for and called to look upon the face of God. There is a kind of homesickness of soul in us that nothing can suppress.

So there we are, sitting by the roadside of life. A world of consumerism has dulled our sight and Jesus of Nazareth is passing by. This is a moment of risk for he can not only pass by; he could pass on and pass us by. On the road to Emmaus, you remember, he made as if "to go on" till the disciples' pressed him to stay; in the storm at sea he started to walk past the boat till they cried out to him. As we sit on the kerbstone of life, he could pass us by for the courtesy of heaven would leave us free. We are free to recognise who he is and then to invite him, or not, into our lives. Jesus of Nazareth is passing by.

At first we cry out "Son of David" but that abstract title begins to burn with deeper significance as we recognise our blindness. Our sins become clearer as he draws close and they force us into a more personal relationship – now it is no longer, "Son of David" but "*Jesus*, have mercy on me". And what do we want? To see again.

There is a moving quality about that "again" as if once, perhaps as children, we saw the truth, saw the face of God in the wonder and surprising gift of this world about us. But now, so much older, we sit by the roadside and Jesus of Nazareth is passing by. He might pass on and our blindness remain. We want to see him again.

So we call out despite the scolding and opposition of a world that crowds about us; we make an effort to throw off something of yesterday's old cloak of living. We come to him, prodigals like the younger son, sinners like the Magdalene, all of us blinded by the sin of the world.

His passing by has stirred in us that call from the Father; that longing for our homeland in heaven. It has brought us to faith, to that "yes" which his courtesy needs if he is to give us true sight and transform our inner life. Jesus of Nazareth is passing by, miraculously close to my small world – in sacrament and in every passing moment of the day.

Blind no longer but contemplating with the eyes of faith, let us, with Bartimaeus, follow him, praising and walking in his footsteps along the way, all along the way to Jerusalem and beyond. For Jesus of Nazareth is passing by.

"Time passing is Christ passing." Each moment is revealing his presence, awaiting our cry lest he pass on and pass us by – "Lord that I may see."

Peter and Paul

"And so we came at last to Rome. And the brethren there, when they heard of us, came as far as the Forum of Appius and Three Taverns to meet us."

(Acts 28:14-15)

As you sit in the Three Taverns, tipping back your tankard, two figures come into view; two curly-haired young men, face to face. You are looking at one of the earliest portraits of saints Peter and Paul, etched into the glass that forms the base of your stoop of ale. A good enough vantage point for reflection on these two pillars of the Church. Though I must admit that the primitive etching can scarcely catch the enormous difference in temperament between the fisherman and the very sophisticated Pharisee.

We first meet St Peter having trouble with his mother-in-law and that endears us at once to our first Pope. A sense of fellowship endures all through his turbulent career from the Lake of Galilee to his upside down crucifixion in Rome. Somehow, Peter's good-natured blundering identifies him with us in a way impossible with St Paul, even when most anguished or indignant on our behalf.

Deep down in St Peter's make-up is, of course, the most kindly and ingrained humility. Few fishermen could have swallowed the directive of a mere carpenter to "stand out into the deep". Fewer still would have blurted out, "depart from me for I am a sinful man," an admission that stirs such a chord in our own grubby hearts. Think how often we have tried to walk on the waters of the spiritual way and started to sink yet gained courage from his heartfelt, "Lord, save me".

Most of us would have foundered at that terrible rebuff – "Get behind me, Satan." Yet when we play Christ false we gain hope from the loyalty of Peter's doglike affection, "Lord, to whom else should we go?" We joke at his terror before the chit of a serving maid but with scourging or crucifixion in the offing – what of us? With all that confusion in the garden would we have struck more accurately than his poor sword stroke that merely sliced off an ear? St Peter's human failings console us – yet beware. There is no room for complacency since his fidelity goes deeper than temperament or culture. It is rooted in an experience that neither we nor St Paul could ever hope to explore.

For St Peter knew Christ the Son of the carpenter years before he realized Christ as the son of the living God. His relationship with Jesus began with something very human. Long before the Prologue's "In the beginning was the Word", long before Philippians' "His nature was from the first divine", St Peter had walked and talked with this attractive young rabbi, never dreaming that at his side was a divine Person. His was St John's initial experience, "what we have heard, what we have seen with our eyes, looked upon and touched with our hands." There were flashes of the incredible truth, "Thou art the Christ, the Son of the living God". There was the glory of the Transfiguration but not until the coming of the Holy Spirit would total realization overwhelm him to proclaim publicly Jesus as Kyrios, Lord.

Somehow the influence of those Galilean days with a Person he took to be just a dear human companion seems to have endured right up to Pentecost and beyond. It colours his speech, humanly, endearingly. "This Jesus, a man attested to you by God..." and it reflects the mind of the early disciples as they tried to cope with the incredible fact of resurrection. Think of the road to Emmaus. "This Jesus of Nazareth who was a prophet (no more than that), a man (just that) mighty in deed and word before God..."

But the colouring goes beyond words for there is a humanity, born of this initial experience of the man, Christ. It is expressed in St Peter's actions – he wept bitterly. Because of this his writings move us more deeply than the Suffering Servant of Isaiah. "Christ himself bore our sins in his body on the tree... By his wounds you have been healed... you were straying like sheep but now have returned to the Shepherd of your souls." First impressions are paramount and the impact of Christ's humanity on Peter never seems to have lost its force from the Jordan to the Tiber.

Something of the same dynamic seems to have energised our own great Apostle, Paul – first encounters, first impressions colouring attitudes that endured through life. Paul had probably never met the Son of the carpenter. He never went fishing with this likeable, though startling, young artisan.

Christ crashed into Paul's world so brilliantly, so powerfully that someone had to lead Paul by the hand, blinded and too dumbfounded to eat for three days. His encounter was with Christ glorified, the son of the living God, whose nature was from the first divine. The starting point here is the realm of the Prologue's "In the beginning was the Word" or the creed's "God from God" or Colossians "first born of all creation". It is a relationship that develops, not from the dusty roads of Galilee, but from one who was in the form of God and only then descends from heaven to the form of a servant, obedient unto death. Paul first met the Person of the risen Lord where St Peter had first chummed up with Christ in his humanity.

It makes a difference to our own relationships. We do feel a kind of homeliness about St Peter as he splashes, weeps and repents before grasping the helm of the Church. And I do not think we would feel so much at ease with St Paul, despite his great Corinthian song of charity. It is not just a matter of the respect that we would feel in the company of any great mind. Rather does it lie in the grounding of his first encounter with the glorified Jesus – first the splendour and only then the Suffering Servant. Like Moses, St Paul comes down to us from the mountain and leaves us a little awed.

First impressions in both apostles have endured through life and yet, when all is said and done, these two saints etched into the base of our tankard, come by different paths to the same conclusions as Mother Church.

St Peter exhorts us to grow up, to ascend from our weak humanity to "share in the divine nature". St Paul urges us to descend from the lofty heights of this "image of the unseen God" to "I live now, not I, but Christ – Christ, crucified – lives in me." But if we really wish to know and live the heights and depths of the beloved master, human and divine, both saints would surely urge us to turn to Mary. She alone has fathomed both; mother of the human infant Child in the crib and mother of the infinite God in heaven.

If we are getting a little high, St Paul brings us down to Christ crucified. If feeling low, St Peter steadies us up, "to whom else should we go – you have the words of eternal life".

St Teresa of Avila

*As we wobble along the narrow way we need a strong
companion, wise in the ways of this world and the next. At
worship or the washing up, the cheerfulness of St Teresa,
foundress of Carmelites, keeps on breaking out. That makes
the going so much the lighter.*

I would like to wish you a very happy feastday for someone
who happens to be my spiritual grandmother as well as
your great foundress – St Teresa of Avila. Years ago my
parents brought to our house a young nun suffering from TB
to convalesce in a small arbour in the garden. She never
recovered but she did leave behind a copy of St Teresa's
autobiography. Somehow, as a teenager, I got hold of it and it
has remained with me ever since.

The book fascinates me. Unlike the Imitation, it is so
cheerful. It is written with the same kind of sweet disarray
that resonates with my own and it seems to make heaven
possible. Later on in life I read that Teresa became a nun with
great determination but without much enthusiasm. That
helped too.

My mother had a great devotion to her but I got the
impression, that as she got older, she switched to the Little
Flower in a desperate attempt to stop smoking. The family
suffered in consequence.

Teresa loved water above "all the other elements" which is
probably why the picture of the woman at the well made such
an impression of her. She guessed that the greatest gift of God
was the Holy Spirit, the torrent of living water flowing from
the side of the king of the golden river. She was always
thirsting for it – "Give me THAT water" and the time came
when the Spirit did come, visibly, to hover over her head like
a silver-winged dove.

She also counted the cost and could compress it into a few
shattering words, "Keep your eyes on the crucified and noth-

ing else will matter much." A short formula for a short way to heaven. A radical way but it never lured her to extremes. "Heaven preserve us from contemplatives like John of the Cross", although this little "half-friar" was dear to her heart.

In a post Vatican II age, where devotion seems to be at a discount, you feel all the more keenly her insistence on the humanity of Christ. "Never, ever lose sight of that." It was a devotion backed up by a desperate hunger for holy communion. On her foundation journeys, flooded rivers, shivering cold, fasting till dusk... nothing could deter her from meeting his majesty there.

And what of us who wander around in the outer rooms of the Interior Castle struggling with all those venomous little creatures? We scarcely hear the pan-pipes of the Shepherd King calling from the innermost and secret chamber of the soul. We can only thank God that we have such a saintly and caring Doctor of the Church – your mother and my spiritual grandmother. There she is promising us the constant presence of Our Lady and St Joseph at the door of our hearts as we wobble along the Way of Perfection.

Let nothing disturb you, nothing dismay you.
All things pass, God never changes.
Patience attains all that it strives for.
He who has God, finds he lacks nothing.
God alone suffices. (Her bookmark)

St George's Day

Once a year a group of elderly veterans, men and women, gather for tea and buns here at the monastery. Some in red berets of the paratroopers, some sporting war medals and some looking so homely and domestic that you would think they had never worn uniform or heard a shot fired.

All of these, in one way or another, have squarely faced death without counting the cost. They come on St George's day for he is the patron of England. His flag flies above the monastery tower whilst we talk, listen and then pray.

WHY MEET? Some time ago, a very kindhearted lady told me she had heard of this annual meeting of veterans at the monastery and wondered why we still went on meeting. Surely it would be better to forget the war, drop these meetings and think about other things.

THE RABBIT. My thoughts went back to a book which told of an old warrior rabbit, his ears torn to shreds from desperate battles, limping from old wounds and an eye poked out from single-handed combat with an evil arch-enemy. Years after, this war-scarred soldier was listening to a couple of bright young things chatting away; "what did they want to fight about? It was all so stupid. You'd think they would have had more sense."

And the old rabbit smiled to himself. Their sense of peace, of security, of the remoteness of war... was the fruit of all his efforts, his wounds and his willingness to give his life that they might live in such serenity. He felt rewarded, even complimented, knowing that peace had once again been won by sweat, blood and tears. No matter if the youngsters would never know the cost.

IF. If the invasion barges were once more gathering across the Channel; if the doodlebugs and V2's were once again terror-

ising our people and the fires of Belsen were still burning –
few would question the sacrifice of so many who gave their
lives or ask why we still meet to honour this day. Few would
wonder why we meet to renew the bond of comradeship,
forged by our common experience and why we want to thank
God for the miracle of a victory that once seemed impossible.

SO. So let us continue to meet; continue to honour those
whose names are inscribed on our war memorials. Above all
let us continue the Christian fight. "For it is not against
human enemies that we have to struggle," St Paul warns us,
but "against the Sovereignties and the Powers who originate
the darkness in this world, the spiritual army of evil in the
heavens. That is why you must rely on God's armour, or you
will not be able to put up any resistance when the worst
happens, or have enough resources to hold your ground." We
are still, it seems, on active service, Christian active service.

> *As you listen to the stories of these veterans and notice their
> war wounds and disabilities, you realise that in some
> mysterious way they have been sharing in the sufferings of
> Christ.*
>
> *They, like him, were willing to lay down their lives for
> their friends out of that greater love which redeems this
> threatened world.*

The Assumption

The annual list for the community feastday sermons tends to ruffle the calm waters of monastic life. You might get Christmas, and that's easy but you might not and then there's panic. Perhaps none greater than for the Assumption. By definition there seems to be nothing on earth to say about this great feast simply because Our Lady has been assumed body and soul into heaven. Saints, after all, have left us relics – a lock of hair or a fragment of bone – but of Our Lady, nothing. And eye has not seen, nor ear heard what goes on up there. It's beyond description, beyond a sermon.

Worse still, the scriptures are not very explicit about this feast and holy pictures of disembodied angels winging Our Lady heavenwards seem to lack conviction. No wonder if that sermon list induces a mild panic.

In Africa, this feast is called "Big Day Maria" and among us Cistercians it is the Big Day of the Year – our patronal feast. I suppose that for some of us it has deep, personal significance – it was, perhaps, the day we came here; the day of profession or of ordination – a very special day. But for all of us it has one happy conclusion. Mary has done what we all hope to do; she has gone home, assumed body and soul into heaven. All her life long she pondered the words of her twelve-year-old son and now she has found him, for ever, in the Temple, in his Father's house.

There is no doubt about this; it is defined dogma and those of us who had reached the age of reason by 1950 are specially proud of it since we had a say in the definition; we were part of the universal assent of the Church. And here, maybe, this sermon should end – with the solid fact of defined dogma for, "Eye hath not seen, nor ear heard, nor has it entered into the heart of man what things God has prepared for those who love him." What more can be said about a mystery that is so barred against human hearing, vision and heart? For myself, I lack the confidence of the small girl at school; "What are you drawing?" said her teacher. "God," came the answer. "You can't do that; no one knows what God looks like. 'When I'm finished, they will'."

A small girl might draw God but I cannot describe Our Lady's assumption and, for this mystery, I fall back on my favourite image of it taken from C.S. Lewis and I hope you will bear with this two and a half minute extract from his classic, *The Great Divorce*.

The reason why I asked if there were another river was this. All down one long aisle of the forest, the under-side of the leafy branches had begun to tremble with dancing light; and on earth I knew nothing so likely to produce this appearance as the reflected light cast upward by moving water. A few moments later I realised my mistake. Some kind of procession was approaching us, and the light came from the persons who composed it.

First came bright Spirits; then on the left and right, at each side of the forest avenue, came youthful shapes, boys on one hand, and girls upon the other. If I could remember their singing and write down the notes, no man who read that score would ever grow sick or old. Between them went musicians; and after these a lady in whose honour all this was being done. And only partly do I remember the unbearable beauty of her face.

"Is it...? is it...?" I whispered to my guide. "Not at all", said he. "It's someone you'll never have heard of. Her name on earth was Sarah Smith and she lived at Golders Green." "She seems to be... well, a person of particular importance." "Aye, she is one of the great ones. You have heard that fame in this country and fame on earth are two quite different things."

"And who are all these young men and women on each side?" "They are her sons and daughters." "She must have had a very large family, Sir." "Every young man or boy that met her became her son – even if it was only the boy that brought the meat to her back door. Every girl that met her was her daughter. Few men looked on her without becoming, in a certain sense, her lovers. But it was the kind of love that made them not less true, but truer, to their own wives."

"And how... but hullo! What are all these animals? A cat – two cats – dozens of cats. And all these dogs... why, I can't count them all. And the birds. And the horses." "They are but her beasts." "Did she keep a sort of zoo? I mean this is a bit too much." "Every beast and bird that came near her had its place in her love. In her they became themselves. And now... the abundance of life she has in Christ from the Father flows over into them."

I looked at my Teacher in amazement. "Yes, it is like when you throw a stone into a pool and the concentric waves spread out further and further. Who knows where it will end? Redeemed humanity is still young, it has hardly come to its full strength.

But already there is joy enough in the little finger of a great saint such as yonder lady to waken all the dead things of the universe into life.

I have always liked that story because it does give some inkling of Our Lady coming into her glory – and I like it more because her homecoming is not just a question of founder's kin. She is mother of God, mother of Jesus – but if kinship to her Son alone brought her up to heaven, then there is not much hope for us poor banished children of Eve.

But it is well for us that Mary, for all her relationship to Christ, took a path that we can tread – for she, like us, lived by faith. It was a faith that found its expression in love. The attractiveness of Lewis's story lies in this – it demonstrates all this in human, accessible ways.

"Every young man or boy that met her, became her son... even if he was only the boy that brought the meat to the back door. In her, they became themselves." First among them was the young man, St John, at the foot of the cross... but the way is also open to us hoary old youngsters, here today. Here is something we can all latch on to – a homely life, lived in faith and love. It is, in fact, with a sense of relief that we hear those hard and testing words of her Son ... insisting that his true family was not just flesh and blood, founder's kin, but discipleship – believing, obedient and loving disciples. "Who are my mother, brothers, sisters ... those who hear the word of God and keep it."

The angel sought Mary out for this faith... Elizabeth blessed her for it ... her calm words at the wedding feast of Cana give some clue to its profundity... and where Jews and Gentiles, kings and politicians all disbelieved... she, to the last, believed at the foot of the cross, though the sword of contradiction and disbelief pierced her heart. In the long procession of all those she is drawing up to heaven, she is the first of the beloved disciples whose faith was expressed and proved in love.

This mystery has set its seal, not only on Mary's soul, but also upon her body and therefore upon all she had been and had done in faith on earth – fetching water, kindling fires, bringing up the child, trudging the roads... all of this has been assumed with her into glory and has been given eternal value. Her triumph has endorsed for us the message of the incarnation... that all our activities do matter, do count. They resonate through all eternity so that what we make of ourselves now, by the grace of God, is what we will be for ever. That gives immense dignity to every passing moment and event and it also means that heaven can start, for us, here below. We are on the way home.

She is already there, thank God. We follow, not by some kind of desperate imitation but because, as Lewis puts it, "The abundance of life she has from the Father, flows from her to us, her children."

In Mary discipleship's faith and motherhood's kinship did indeed coincide and by the grace of this mystery of the Assumption, the same is happening to us.

She is winning for us the power to become children of God as we believe in the name of her Son with a faith that is finding its expression in love.

As we come round on the beads to the Assumption what thoughts, what image arise to drive off the buzzing distractions of earthly life? They usually win out and yet this mystery still generates in us a quiet hope. Flesh and blood, the likes of us, are already there in heaven. It is a place real enough to be home to this glorious human being. At Medjugorge, they say people were invited to touch her and their hands met with solid resistance. Hope springs from the fact that she has gone home and put the kettle on. She waits, not just for the great ones like Sarah Smith of Golders Green, but also for you and me.

And this hope grows before the sheer power of this mystery. Think of a whirlwind sucking heavenwards everything in its path – leaves, trees, dustbins, the Monday washing – all swirling up into the sky. Perhaps Our Lady sweeps us home like this for she is a whirlwind of mothering love.

The Snow Queen

Liturgical experts have axed a most attractive feastday –
Our Lady of the Snows. To mark the site of a church and
in the heat of an Italian summer she sent a fall of snow on
the hillside. A feastday now suppressed but in fact
irrepressible for nothing so evokes and befits Mary
Immaculate as white and sunlit snow.

Who knows
    where she goes
Mary, Mother of the Snows?

        How well
        All can tell
        Heaven and Earth –
        Save only Hell.

In snows
All shows
Whoever comes, whoever goes.

        Maiden's purity piercing white
        Mantles the earth, whereon the sight,
        Press of her foot,
        A tread so light.

Her spell
All can tell,
Heaven and Earth,
save only Hell.

"And you frost and snow, O bless the Lord.
To him be highest glory and praise for ever."

Bill

The Pope is urging us, as never before, to spread the Good News. Today he dreams of calling Moslems, Jews and Catholics to a summit conference atop Mount Sinai by the year 2000. But how on earth go about it?

People, as a rule, are all agog to hear the latest news, good or bad, and sometimes you notice them glancing at their watches round about 6 pm, edging away to get to the news. But when it comes to really good news, eternal life and happiness, won by the cross of Christ, a glazed look comes into the eye and they begin to feel embarrassed. And you wonder how to evangelise, how to speak of heaven to a comfortable first world or, more difficult still, how bring good news to the suffering, to those millions of refugees in Rwanda?

It is something I have often pondered and my admiration goes out to those missionaries who take up the task so joyfully. A friend, faintly interested in the faith, backed off when I mentioned the RCIA course and if you go for something simpler like the penny Catechism, then note that there are 390 questions. Few have the stamina for that. To preach by example is sound advice but, looking at all the nasty things in the woodshed of our souls, somehow the stuffing goes out of us.

Vatican II has suggested that we appreciate our sister churches and profit by their good qualities. This came home to me some years ago when standing with one of the brothers in Gatwick airport, waiting to see home an African monk. A big, friendly man started talking to us and in a matter of minutes was telling us about eternal life in a most interesting and engaging fashion. He turned out to be a famous evangelist, Bill Bright. His special mission was in the difficult area of American teenage students. As we were leaving he pulled out of his pocket a minute booklet, about 2" x 3", called the Four Spiritual Laws. It had run to millions of copies so you felt that it must have something relevant to say about evangelisation. From a Catholic point of view it is incomplete but it does give a lead-in to this difficult task.

Law One touches those millions who feel there is no meaning, no incentive to life. Quite simply it says, "God loves you and has a plan for your life." How be so sure of this? Well, "he so loved the world that he did not spare his only Son but gave him up for us all" – there's the love and then comes the plan, "That all who believe in him... should have eternal life." If this sounds too good to be true, listen to the Son – "I came that they might have life and have it more abundantly."

We may wonder why such a plan of eternal happiness brings so little reaction, so little joy. Law Two bluntly answers. We have sinned, we are distanced from God and can scarcely experience his loving designs for us. If you offend a human friend, affection and communication begin to falter. So what if we offend the living God? Scripture says that "All men have sinned and fall short of the glory of God" and the "wages of sin is death". Little wonder if there is so little response. Joy cannot co-exist with death but, luckily for us, God is not a human friend. He is divinely determined upon our happiness.

He has sent his Son precisely to call sinners, to heal the sick in soul; he has "made provision" for us as Law Three quaintly puts it. Jesus Christ is God's only provision for our sinfulness. "While we were yet sinners", says St Paul, "Christ died for us", died for our sins and rose for our justification. He is the only way back to God, "the way, the truth and the life; no one comes to the Father but by me".

Here, perhaps, comes the crunch of Law Four, which is our response to the Father's loving designs. We must receive Jesus Christ as our Lord and Saviour because "as many as received him, to them he gave the power to become children of God, to those who believe in his name". Christ stands at the door of our hearts and knocks. If we, through faith, open that door then "I will come to him" and eternal life is ours. Our heart is a throne and if we enthrone him there, by a faith that finds expression in love, then his Kingdom is come and the work begun.

Spreading the good news is difficult and Bill Bright knew little about the rich sacramental life of the Church but, if those four laws are somehow in mind, at least we shall have a well of living water to draw upon.

1. God has a loving plan for each one of us.
2. Sinfulness bars and blinds us to it.
3. His Son is the provision that can heal us.
4. We make our response to such good news by the gift of faith.

Four laws, easy to remember and packing great punch as Bill demonstrated in a matter of minutes at a busy, crowded airport.